The Information Society: Issues and Answers

The Information Society: Issues and Answers

American Library Association's Presidential Commission for the 1977 Detroit Annual Conference

Edited with a Preface and Introduction by E.J. Josey and a Foreword by Clara Stanton Jones

A Neal-Schuman Professional Book

ORYX PRESS
Mansell London
1978

Operation Oryx, started more than 10 years ago at the Phoenix Zoo to save the rare white antelope—believed to have inspired the unicorn of mythology—has apparently succeeded.

An original herd of nine, put together through Operation Oryx by five world organizations, now numbers 34 in Phoenix with another 22 farmed out to the San Diego Wild Game Farm.

The operation was launched in 1962 when it became evident that the animals were facing extinction in their native habitat of the Arabian peninsula.

Copyright © 1978 by E. J. Josey
Published by The Oryx Press
3930 E. Camelback Road
Phoenix, AZ 85018

Published simultaneously in Canada

All rights reserved
No part of this publication may be reproduced or transmitted in any form or by any means, electronic or mechanical, including photocopying, recording, or by any information storage and retrieval system, without permission in writing from The Oryx Press

Printed and Bound in the United States of America

Distributed outside North America by
Mansell Information/Publishing Limited
3 Bloomsbury Place
London WC1A 2QA, England
ISBN 0-7201-0823-3

Library of Congress Cataloging in Publication Data

Main entry under title:

The Information Society: issues and answers.

    (A Neal-Schuman professional book)
    Includes index.
    1. Libraries and society — Congress.
2. Information science — Congress. I. Josey, E. J., 1924 — II. American Library Association. President's Commission on the Detroit Congress.
Z672.5.I54   021   78-17708
ISBN 0-912700-16-5

*Dedicated
to the
Memory
of*
*ELIZABETH T. FAST
a
Library Media Specialist*

*whose enormous professional contributions and
enthusiasm aided us substantially in our
understanding of the information society*

Contents

Foreword *Clara Stanton Jones*   ix
Preface *E. J. Josey*   xi
Introduction *E. J. Josey*   xiv
Notes on Contributors   xix

Prologue: Post-Industrial Society and the Growth of Information: The Impact on Libraries *Rollin Marquis*   1

To Give a Nation Soul *Norman E. Isaacs*   4

The Impact of Technology on Libraries *Frederick G. Kilgour*   12

The Impact of Technology on Libraries and Librarians: A Literature Review *Susan K. Martin*   20

The Impact of Social Change on Libraries *Major Owens*   26

The Impact of Social Change on Libraries: A Literature Review *Leigh Estabrook and Thomas Blumenthal*   36

The Impact of Economic Change on Libraries *Thomas R. Buckman*   47

The Impact of Economic Change on Libraries: A Review of the Literature *William W. Sannwald*   63

The New Role of the Librarian in the Information Age *Gerald R. Shields*   75

The New Role of Librarians as Professionals: A Literature Review *Thomas J. Galvin, Barbara Immroth, Margaret Mary Kimmel, Desretta V. McAllister, and James M. Matarazzo*   80

Public Access to Information in the Post-Industrial Society *Fay M. Blake*   86

Literature on Problems of Access in Libraries *Miriam Braverman*   94

Epilogue: Issues and Answers: The Participants' Views *Joseph A. Boissé and Carla J. Stoffle*   110

Index *Sanford Berman*   123

Foreword

Every generation considers its problems to be the most difficult ever faced by mankind. Indeed, the claim of each era in its turn would be hard to refute. The unique claim of our era to this distinction is not only our phenomenal scientific and technological development, but the resulting unmatched rapidity of change. Individuals and institutions alike are caught up in the historic gallop. Libraries and the library profession are inextricably involved in the "information explosion," the "publishing explosion," and all the attendant repercussions that are hallmarks of a sophisticated technological society. As librarians, we must appreciate the importance of our involvement. Along with all other segments of society we are faced with the choice of confronting both old and new situations and problems. We must not continue to dodge and muddle through. The temptation of the latter is especially great because of the aggravation and discouragement of recurring economic recessions. The goal is to assess public information needs vis-à-vis the library profession's potential and to harness appropriate technology for the delivery of effective library service. This requires careful study and planning, continuing exchange of ideas and points of view, and a deep understanding of the interrelated human problems of contemporary society.

The "Issues and Answers" program at the 1977 annual American Library Association conference identified some major concerns and involved about 1500 librarians in grappling with a few selected issues of primary importance to all. It was not easy to make a choice from the long list of ideas that emerged when the planning committee engaged in a "brainstorming" session. However, in one way or another, all suggested topics related to the impact of technology and the accompanying economic and social change. It became evident that librarians must address these common causal factors in order to understand specific problems and place them in proper perspective. Thus, the tripartite subject of the "Issues and Answers" program seemed to choose itself—"The Impact of Technological, Social and Economic Change on Libraries." But, the subject was incomplete without practical application. It seemed logical to build the right of access to information into the framework of the "Issues and Answers." It also seemed necessary to give attention to the new role of librarians as professionals as they respond to powerful forces of change.

It cannot be said that the program accomplished all it intended but, hopefully, it contributed to a commitment to confront our professional problems and opportunities and to *think* our way through the demands of change. It is hoped that through the publication of these papers, we may share these "Issues and Answers" with the entire profession.

Clara Stanton Jones, Director
Detroit Public Library

Preface

The Information Society: Issues and Answers is a collection of eight essays on critical issues with which librarians and information specialists must grapple as we move further into the post-industrial society. In addition, there are five literature review papers designed as a bibliographical road map for further exploration into the ramifications of the multitude of perplexing problems of the information society. As the reader delves into the ideas and concepts presented by the authors of the essays, I am confident that what will emerge in his or her consciousness is that the information society is today, and not necessarily off in a distant future. What will also become evident is that in spite of the bewitchment of technology and the way it has transformed the world with its dazzling technological prospects, the writers of the issue papers have not forgotten human needs in the post-industrial society.

The volume is organized to give the flavor of the President's Program and the papers are presented herewith in the order of their presentation followed by their literature review paper. Rollin Marquis' paper used by the discussion leaders for their training session at the 1977 midwinter meeting, "Post-Industrial Society and the Growth of Information: The Impact on Society," serves as the prologue. Marquis concludes his paper by indicating that "the potentiality of serving an ever-growing proportion of the population seems to become more apparent with every year we move into the post-industrial society."

Norman E. Isaacs, in his essay "To Give a Nation Soul," discusses the problems of communications and links libraries to similar difficulties. He rebukes librarians who are willfully unresponsive to community needs. Urging librarians to plug into the new communications systems, Isaacs admonishes that "libraries are going to become working community centers. . . ." One of his most quotable quotes for *The Information Society: Issues and Answers* is that "nothing in life is now more important than that the flow of information remain uncontaminated."

Frederick G. Kilgour's "Impact of Technology on Libraries" reviews the history of libraries and technology and advises that "the computerized library network has had little effect on patrons of libraries, but the next decade will surely witness dramatic improvement in the ability of patrons to obtain needed information from libraries." Susan K. Martin's literature review of the subject provides a discussion of thirty-four sources which give further insight into this intriguing subject.

"The Impact of Social Change on Libraries," by New York State Senator Major Owens is a challenge to the profession of librarianship. Speaking about the sins of omissions of librarians and their failure to respond to social change, Senator Owens declares that "as time has woven an increasingly complex social fabric, certain threads and strands were left out because librarians did not step forward to weave in that portion . . . that only librarians knew how to include." In his prescription for the future, he calls for increased mastery of the political and public policy-making process and urges librarians to use the White House Conference as a vehicle to capture the attention of the American public on behalf of libraries. The review paper on social change by Leigh Estabrook and Thomas Blumenthal identifies thirty sources, grouped under three categories: "general works on the subject; works that consider the impact of social change on the library profession; and works that study the impact of social change on library and information services."

Thomas R. Buckman's "The Impact of Economic Change on Libraries" focuses attention on one of the most critical issues that librarians face currently and in the years ahead. Buckman offers the sobering thought that "libraries are beginning to benefit by economies of scale . . . but inevitably when there are more users there must be higher materials budgets and more service staff and, therefore, costs expand in proportion to the number of people served. Success in meeting information needs may also, ironically, result in larger deficits given the present structure of libraries." William W. Sannwald's literature review paper cites fifty-nine sources, under nine rubrics, that the reader may wish to investigate: productivity, human resources, unionism, library materials, library cooperation, energy, technology, funding sources, and budgeting techniques.

Gerald R. Shields analyzes the effect of rapid technological change on the role of the librarian. Rather than being frightened by the new technology, Shields believes that "the librarian should be acting as an information transfer agent. The librarian must be allowed to fulfill an advocacy role in the utilization of information technology. If information is our *infinite* resource, then the ability to utilize the finite physical resources most assuredly depends upon information technology and the librarian."

Thomas J. Galvin, Barbara Immroth, Margaret Mary Kimmel, Desretta V. McAllister, and James M. Matarazzo in their literature review essay on the new role of librarians as professionals cite thirty-five references for further study of this important subject. The references were reviewed under three categories: Relationships with Clients, Relationships with Institutions, and Relationships with the Profession.

"Public Access to Information in the Post-Industrial Society" by Fay M. Blake is an animated, intellectually stimulating and critical analysis of the problems confronting librarians relative to public access to information. Blake contends that "all people need information but the kinds of information most people need are different in form and content from that required and made available by the educated elite." Probing the numerous barriers to access to information, Blake also feels that librarians have helped to create barriers as evidenced by her penetrating comment: "Librarians have lent themselves to that restrictive aspect of information gathering and dissemination. Out of a combination of timidity, snobbery, ignorance and miseducation, we have never spoken for the right of *everyone* to information." The review paper on "The Literature on Problems of Access in Libraries," by Miriam Braverman, provides seventy-six sources described under the subject categories of: On-line Services; The Budget Crunch and a New Look at Organization and Practices; Networking; The Information-Rich and the Information-Poor; Information and Referral Systems; The Right to Know and the Right to Be Left Alone; and Censorship/Intellectual Freedom.

The last essay, "Issues and Answers: The Participants' Views" by Joseph A. Boissé and Carla J. Stoffle is the epilogue. The authors of this essay distilled comments and ideas from thousands of 3x5 cards to provide a comprehensive and panoramic view of the results of this all-day conference within a conference. Boissé and Stoffle identified four recurring themes:

> A serious uncertainty about the role of the librarian . . . a continued malaise about library education . . . a deep-seated fear of the uncertainty of the future which is brought on by changing economic conditions . . . [and] exasperation with the lack of planning and coordination . . . in the library world.

Was the President's Program successful? Boissé and Stoffle found that "almost to an individual, the participants expressed not only a sense of satisfaction with the program, but an appreciation for the opportunity presented by the program."

In the preparation of a volume of papers from a conference for publication, an editor is inevitably faced with the question of what to cut down. I have taken a fairly liberal approach and attempted to preserve, insofar as possible, the full text except for minor circumlocution that creeps into oral communications. However, I have inserted subtopics to aid the reader. At the same time I have purposely made an effort to preserve the flavor of the talks as they were presented at the President's Program.

While I am deeply indebted to Arthur Curley, Patricia Glass Schuman, and Gerald R. Shields, who gave invaluable assistance as members of the subcommittee who aided in the selection of the speakers, and especially for their editorial advice, only I am responsible for the editorial errors or interpretations that may surface in this volume.

E. J. Josey
Albany, New York
February, 1978

Introduction

Development of the President's Program: The Genesis of an Idea

by E. J. Josey

The 1977 annual conference of the American Library Association was not envisioned as the usual yearly conference. It was the first annual conference to follow the Association's centennial celebration. What do the planners of an important event such as the President's Program develop as a substantive theme, following a grand and colossal centenary celebration? What are the most pressing issues facing the Association? What is the best program format that would encourage the active participation of hundreds of ALA members? These were major questions facing Acting President Clara Stanton Jones[1] as she planned her year of the ALA presidency 1976-77.

In her usual creative manner, on May 15, 1976, Acting President Jones assembled a group of eleven persons as a Presidential Commission. She invited the members of this group, including Augusta Baker, David R. Bender, Mary K. Chelton, Miriam Crawford, Arthur Curley, Connie R. Dunlap, E. J. Josey, Frederick Kilgour, Annette L. Phinazee, Patricia Glass Schuman, and Gerald Shields to a one-day conference at the LaGuardia Airport Conference Center.

The primary reasons for Ms. Jones' developing scenario employing the use of a "Presidential Commission" to assist her in the planning of the "President's Program" are clearly stated in her invitation to the members of the Association to serve on the august body:

---

1 Because of the untimely death of President Allie Beth Martin, the ALA Executive Board at its Spring 1976 meeting appointed Vice President/President-Elect Jones Acting President.

This Commission will plan and carry out the day-long "Issues and Answers" program to be held during the 1977 ALA conference in Detroit — my version of the traditional "President's Program." The first meeting of the Commission will take place in New York City on Saturday, May 15, at the LaGuardia Airport Conference Center in Fiorello-A Room from 10 a.m. to 6 p.m. . . .

The "Issues and Answers" program will commence on Monday evening, June 20, 1977, with a keynote speaker. The next day, the extremely large Riverside Ballroom in Cobo Hall will be utilized for the all-day, self-contained meeting. People will be seated at round tables that hold ten, with a group leader and recorder at each table. Not more than four "issues" will be presented during the course of the day. The issues are to be determined by the Commission with sensitivity to membership interests. Assuming that there will be two sessions in the morning and two in the afternoon, one-half hour will be allotted for presentation of each issue, followed by an hour's discussion at the tables. The emphasis will be on the use of ALA membership talent, although outside speakers can be invited where appropriate. The four (?) "Issue" presentation papers are to be circulated in advance to the chairperson and to each table discussion leader in order that all can be well prepared for their roles. Also, leaders will be asked to participate in a session on group discussion dynamics to insure good interaction. Table recorders will be asked to take notes and prepare a summary by the end of the Conference that will become part of an overall summary of the day. . . .

If the concept described above proves to be feasible, a sizeable number of members will take important responsibility in the implementation, and a large number of members in attendance will participate in the program itself. Program content should reflect membership concerns. Very careful advance planning will be required, with the President's Commission at the helm. I am inviting only the above named persons to this initial meeting, but by the July conference, the Commission will be enlarged somewhat to be reasonably representative of the Association, geographically and otherwise. The need is imperative for this meeting to be held before July; consequently, in the interest of time and transportation constraints, everyone comes from east of Chicago for this May meeting.

By the July 1976 Annual Conference, Acting President Jones had appointed the following additional persons to serve on the Commission: Wyman Jones, Donald Roberts, Ernest Siegel, Elizabeth Martinez Smith, Roderick Swartz, and Herman Totten. Other ALA leaders, who were not members of the Commission, attended the July 1976 Planning Sessions; these persons included Elizabeth Fast, Alice B. Ihrig, and Eric Moon.

The members of the Commission began to consider their responsibility, and it soon became apparent that the 1977 Annual Conference would be the "first step into ALA's second century." As they attempted to forecast the future of libraries, information, and society by the year 2000, one of the recurring themes in the discussion was technological change. Patricia Glass Schuman uttered the major words. She raised the question: Why don't we consider "Libraries and the Post-Industrial Society?" The concept of the post-industrial society seeped into our consciousness and found fertile soil. The lengthy unstructured free-flowing discussion of technological change and its multiplicity of possible effects and implications, and what it might portend for the future, led us to accept the realization that the controllers of technology will control America's future.

Members of the Commission, in further analyzing the situation of libraries and society by the end of the century, discussed the eminent sociologist, Daniel Bell, and his observations in his 1973 book, *The Coming of Post-Industrial Society, A Venture in Social Forecasting.* Bell sees post-industrial society crystallizing some thirty to forty years in the future. He contends that society is at the start of a new stage in its development, in which the dominant activity is not the production of goods or food but the provision of information and services. The United States has already become the first country in which more than half the work force is employed in activities other than manufacture or agriculture. Concurrently, knowledge is multiplying at a rapid rate. Technology transforms agriculture to reduce the number of people involved in the production of food to a mere four percent of the work force, and manufacturing is becoming similarly automated. The service economy will change the nature of the work force so that white collar occupations outnumber blue collar occupations. With society becoming highly technologically skilled and recondite, education, according to Bell, is the mode of access to power.

From the foregoing discussion of Bell's ideas, it was obvious that the United States was rapidly becoming the "Information Society." Commission member Gerald R. Shields admonished the group to ponder Edwin B. Parker's ideas:

> Information, rather than labor or capital, is becoming the key factor in production. Peter Drucker argues, "Knowledge, during the last few decades has become the central capital, the cost center, and the crucial resource of the economy . . ." Servan-Schreiber, in *American Challenge*, outlines what he sees as the United States' threat of economic domination of Western Europe as essentially an information advantage. The recent Japanese "white paper" titled *The Plan for Information Society - A National Goal Toward Year 2000* recommends a major, centrally planned development of what they call "the information society." They propose a five-year investment of 1,000 billion yen (3.2 billion dollars). Their argument is that with such a national investment they can sustain an annual rate of growth of GNP in excess of ten percent per year, contrasted with a seven percent growth rate if they follow a U.S. style of laissez-faire policy of information investment.[2]

Following the Commission's meeting during the 1976 annual conference, President Jones appointed a subcommittee to choose five speakers and serve as a committee to review and edit their papers. Arthur Curley, Patricia Glass Schuman, and Gerald R. Shields were named to the committee with this writer chosen as Chairperson.

After the selection of a keynote speaker, five distinguished librarians were chosen to speak at the all-day session of the "Issues and

---

2 Parker, Edwin B. "Information Society," in *Annual Review of Information Science and Technology.* 8:351 (1973).

Answers" program. Knowledgeable professionals were then chosen to prepare reviews of the literature papers that would be placed in every conferee's registration packet.

As plans continued to crystallize, 150 persons were chosen as discussion leaders. Annette L. Phinazee was responsible for developing an orientation session for discussion leaders at the 1977 ALA midwinter meeting. Barbara Conroy, because of her expertise in leadership education, was invited to serve as the Leader of the Midwinter Workshop on the Dynamics of Group Discussion. A background paper prepared by Rollin Marquis, which introduced the "Issues and Answers" topic, served as a point of departure for the workshop. The discussion leaders' training session was very successful, thereby contributing to the overall success of the program at the Detroit Conference.

On Monday evening, June 20th, the plenary session of the President's Program began with President Clara Stanton Jones presiding. Governor William G. Milliken and other state and city officials were present to greet the conferees. It was heart-warming for the huge throng to have been greeted by Governor Milliken, not only because he had recently signed a $27.8 million state aid bill for Detroit, of which one-fifth was for the Detroit Public Library, but also for his reassuring words on the growing importance of libraries to the economic, educational and social good of the community, and more importantly, how much he valued the commitment of librarians.

The keynote speaker for the occasion was a specialist in communications, Norman Isaacs, Editor-in-Residence, School of Journalism, Columbia University. Underscoring the importance of libraries to him personally, Isaacs indicated that "I got my education in the free library." His address set the stage for the all-day program on the following day.

On Tuesday morning, June 21, 1977, 150 discussion leaders arrived at Cobo Hall in Detroit at 8:00 a.m.—one hour before the beginning of the program for the purpose of receiving their final briefing and instructions. I chaired this session and reviewed with the group the three major goals of the President's Program. Its primary goal was to promote discussion on topics affecting the future of librarianship and library and information services. The five speakers were to react to the issues, clarify and define the critical questions and project into the future. The discussion leaders were reminded that their goal was to be both facilitator and catalyst—to promote information exchange and a sharing of opinion and viewpoint. Although recommendations for future action might emerge during the discussion, this was not necessarily a primary goal.

More than 1,500 registrants appeared at the Cobo Hall Ballroom at 9:00 a.m. The day-long President's Program, "Issues and Answers—The Information Society" commenced. Arthur Curley, a member of the Presidential Commission, chaired the event. In his opening remarks, he described the gathering as "the world's largest reactor panel" and compared the undertaking to the 1963 ALA Conference within a Conference. It was indeed a conference within a conference and the "world's largest reactor panel"; the 1,500 persons, with their trained discussion leaders at tables throughout the mammoth ballroom, participated in discussion periods following each of five addresses. During the course of the day two persons were assigned the responsibility of "floating" from table to table to listen to the discussion and to pick up the reactions and recommendations from the participants. During the last period in the day, I took over the gavel once more from Curley and introduced Joseph A. Boissé and Carla J. Stoffle, who presented the participants' views and gave a summary. At 6:00 p.m. the participants began to leave Cobo Hall's Ballroom indicating that this had been a "mind-boggling" experience.

The foregoing account of the development of the President's Program and the scenario as it unfolded serves as a backdrop for the illuminating and provocative papers that were prepared and are presented in this volume.

Notes on Contributors

Fay M. Blake is a member of the faculty of the School of Library and Information Studies, University of California, Berkeley.

Thomas Blumenthal is a graduate student, Simmons College, Boston.

Joseph A. Boissé is Director of the Library/Learning Center, University of Wisconsin-Park Side.

Miriam Braverman is Assistant Professor, School of Library Services, Columbia University.

Thomas R. Buckman is President of the Foundation Center, New York City.

Leigh Estabrook is Associate Professor, School of Information Studies, Syracuse University.

Thomas J. Galvin is Professor and Dean, Graduate School of Library and Information Science, University of Pittsburgh.

Barbara Immroth is a doctoral student at the Graduate School of Library and Information Science, University of Pittsburgh.

Norman E. Isaacs is Associate Dean and Editor-in-Residence, Graduate School of Journalism, Columbia University.

Clara Stanton Jones is Past President of the American Library Association and Retired Director of the Detroit Public Library.

E. J. Josey is Chief, Bureau of Specialist Library Services, Library Development, New York State Education Department.

Frederick G. Kilgour is Director, Ohio College Library Center.

Margaret Mary Kimmel is a Visiting Lecturer and doctoral student, Graduate School of Library and Information Science, University of Pittsburgh.

Desretta V. McAllister is a doctoral student, Graduate School of Library and Information Science and member of the faculty, School of Library Science, North Carolina Central University.

Rollin Marquis is Chief Librarian, Department of Libraries, Dearborn, Michigan.

Susan K. Martin is Head, Library Systems Office, University of California, Berkeley and President-Elect of the Information Science and Automation Division of the American Library Association.

James M. Matarazzo is a doctoral student at the Graduate School of Library and Information Science, University of Pittsburgh.

Major Owens is a member of the New York State Senate, a member of the New York Governor's Commission on Libraries and lectures at the School of Library Service, Columbia University.

William W. Sannwald is Associate Director for Support Services, Detroit Public Library.

Gerald R. Shields is Assistant Professor and Assistant Dean, School of Information and Library Studies, State University of New York at Buffalo.

Carla J. Stoffle is Assistant Director, Library/Learning Center, University of Wisconsin-Park Side.

The Information Society: Issues and Answers

Prologue

Post-Industrial Society and the Growth of Information: The Impact on Libraries

by Rollin Marquis

"Post-industrial society," a term coined by Daniel Bell and now in wide use, suggests that presently evolving society, in the areas of the world which have become highly industrialized, is increasingly characterized by having its labor force concentrated in the sphere of services, professional and technical, rather than in the sphere of extractive industries—agriculture, mining, fishing, forestry—characteristic of pre-industrial society; or in the sphere of manufacturing and distributive industries, characteristic of industrial society—including, until recently, our own.

From another perspective, the term suggests that our society will more and more be marked by interaction between persons, rather than between people and nature or between people and the fabricated means of processing the resources of nature.

Our primary institutions are expected to be the university, the academic institute, the research corporation, the industrial laboratory, the library; our economic ground, science-based industries; our primary resource, human capital; our political problem, science policy and education policy; our structural problem, the balancing of the interests of the public and private sectors.

Upward access through the social-economic strata of this society is assumed to depend upon advanced education even more than at present.

Resistance to bureaucracy, claiming of social rights, determination of social policy, and demands for social and economic benefits may increasingly be effected by collective negotiation or action through participatory citizen movements, communities of interest, pressure groupings of the class action and advocacy type.

This political process may by no means necessarily be amiable, even peaceable; confrontations of communities of interest may often be of an adversary nature. Tendencies which will inspire opposition may well be those toward centralization, bureaucratization; manipulation of the individual and invasion of privacy, elitism and meritocracy; and the limiting of upward social and economic mobility to the route of formal training and formal acquisition of skills.

The widening role of science-based industry and research institutes should sustain a continuing increase in serial and monographic publication, which may expand dramatically with the growth of universities and scientific institutions in previously pre-industrial nations.

Dissemination of published information would be assisted by the anticipated appearance of inexpensive, high-capacity, world-wide, two-way or conference communication, including video communication; rapid reproduction, transmission and reception of visual information, including facsimile transmission; widespread access to computers for intellectual and professional assistance, at home and in libraries as well as in schools and workplaces.

Video, computerized, and programmed learning may make study feasible at any location, including libraries, and in so doing may affect the function of libraries by making them much more apparently educational institutions.

And of course the expansion and refinement of telecommunications may make possible obtaining information from libraries audiotaped; videotaped; printed or video displayed as a reference, citation or abstract; or reproduced as a list of references, bibliography or facsimile; and more important, obtaining such information by remote access without dependence on transportation to visit a library facility. This in turn could imply that libraries might need less space to accommodate users while being able to house or have direct access to much greater collections because of advanced techniques of storing, retrieving, reproducing and transmitting information.

Even with computer-stored and microform-recorded information, however, the expense of acquiring, handling and housing information is expected to increase and add its weight to the pressure of the logic of interlibrary sharing and exchange. But a national program for libraries will have many obstacles to overcome, especially jurisdictional arrangements and local funding practices. Some forecasts occur of the establishment of a comprehensive national pool (or a very few regional pools) of serial and monographic resources. Others announce the coming of a nation-wide division among existing libraries of acquisition responsibility for designated subject fields; networking in the sense of library-resource sharing and the provision of information service through telecommunications is likely to grow continuously, regardless, because of the ever-enlarging volume of information and the overall cost of handling it.

At the same time as we see increased importance placed on higher, professional and technical education, we may expect to see more emphasis placed on individualized education, not tied to textbook, lecture and classroom contexts; more of a trend from formal teaching toward computer-based education utilizing planned inquiry. Such an educational mode is projected to require much more intensive use of library resources.

While the way to social advancement and economic betterment may be more narrowly confined to the attainment of learning and the acquisition of skills, the new mode of education is purported to be both more reasonable and more equitable, because it would give all students equal treatment, at their preferred pace, via their individual inclinations to inquiry.

But the notion of technology assisting learning would be theoretical unless access to the means of distributing information were unimpeded and inexpensive. Here should be a primary role for libraries; and, more important, for librarians, who have a long tradition of dealing with the users of information on an individual basis.

Our profession in the future may be oriented yet more than today away from clerical and technical routines, even those still classed as "intellectual" functions, and toward the selection and arrangement of materials *for use* and the assistance and instruction of users.

It has been observed that those who can read and have been exposed to printed sources of knowledge have an advantage over the illiterate in our form of society, in every area of learning and social interaction. And it has often been the comment that access to timely, accurate, well-organized information is the key to effective decision making, letting those with the means, know-how, and ability to acquire that information, benefit most from the results of having acquired it.

In principle, the knowlege fund of our society is stored in our libraries, which have served a relatively small proportion of our citizens. The potentiality of serving an ever-growing proportion of the population seems to become more apparent with every year as we move into a post-industrial society.

To Give A Nation Soul

by Norman E. Isaacs

INTRODUCTION

For a considerable period I was in a state of frustration over what I could say that might be meaningful. Because ethics—the application of moral and intellectual principles—has been my major interest for well over three decades, I kept seeking some extensions into your own appraisals of the emerging post-industrial society.

Then it came to me that the ethical tie to your new, vital roles in the coming society lies in the inscription on the Archives Building in Washington, D.C.: "What is past is prologue."

As you know, I am a member of the senior faculty of what is generally regarded as the most distinguished graduate school of its kind in the world. I have been fortunate enough to have been accorded almost every honor journalism has to bestow. I have no degree of any kind—not even a high school diploma. But my education has been sound, solid and broad. It all came from the free libraries. And while today I have my own excellent technical collection, I continue to rely on the resources of the libraries within my reach.

My heart goes out to all who struggle against the constraints of today's America because when I think back fifty-two years to when I got my first newspaper job, the realization of how vastly everything has changed is staggering.

I was foreign-born—and resident only three years in a city that boasted publicly that more than ninety-five percent of its citizens were native-born. I bore a Jewish name in a city patently WASP-run. The newspaper required no application form and no test. The only thing needed was a work permit that I had obtained in ten minutes at City Hall. One glance by the editor at the permit and I was embarked on a career.

It didn't take long for me to discover how ignorant I was about a vast range of subjects. Newspaper libraries in those days were only of marginal help. No wonder they were called morgues! So other than finding people who knew intimately the background data I needed, the public library became my second office and home.

How does one retrace how one picks and chooses reading material? It is all hazy now. I do know that a city police scandal got me into Lincoln Steffens; that led to Ida Tarbell, and the other great muckrakers. My interest in newspapers led me into books about Greeley, Hearst, Pulitzer—and one of the great influences of my life— Walter Lippmann. It was reading Lippmann that spread me to history and law and philosophy. Lippmann alone was sufficient to give me a sense of conscience about what it was I was into as a journalist.

Twelve years after the beginning day, I was a managing editor—a boy editor, immensely proud of his calling but dissatisfied with its reach, its scope, its goals. I was developing a love-hate relationship. It became more defined as the years matured me. I often reproach my calling because it has not and does not live up to its promise—and in some instances not even up to its duty. So I often sound like a common scold about something very dear to me; very dear because the opportunities for public service through communications are enormous.

Many of you in the parallel communications field of library work harbor similar schizoid feelings about your profession. Don't be ashamed of it. It is what progress is built upon. If you are to build the kinds of new library services needed to better serve your constituencies, you must be constantly aware of where you are falling short— and, most important, you must have an ethical conviction about what it is you are undertaking.

COMMUNICATIONS PROBLEMS

Detroit in itself offers a classic case study of our many, differing communications problems. It epitomizes all of our current traumas—a major urban center caught in the throes of both recession and inflation; manufacturing and union selfishness; educational systems in disrepair; massive welfare loads in a zone where the tax base has eroded dramatically; housing a disgrace; and, over the whole, all too many evidences of mismanagement of the public business by political bureaucracies; and entirely too much self-seeking by one and all.

We suffer from huge rents in the imaginary tent we had constructed—the one Denis Brogan called our "myth of omnipotence."

More than a few believe that the United States may have entered the waning phase among world societies. Certainly, unless some major changes take place within the next two decades, we run the risk that the societal dysfunctions will have become so immense that there may be no way to reverse disintegration.

While I recognize the dangers, I do not join with the pessimists. The three-legged base for what goes on in this nation is, for me, government, the law, and communications.

Where government is concerned, it seems to me that too many of our public officials have not yet caught up with the meaning of the last election. They appear to be indulging in business as usual, playing with patronage, logrolling and indulging in word games.

What the majority of the American people in the last election was saying was that they want the negative drift halted. They elected as President a man they knew precious little about—but whom they decided was expressing what they felt was inside themselves.

If this is a correct extrapolation, they were saying as they voted that they were fed up to the gills with a governmental apparatus that is self-serving, grasping of every conceivable fringe benefit, and amoral about its functions, if not immoral. What they seemed to me to be saying also was that they are ashamed of the injustices so evident in today's society.

Few of these citizens who voted for Jimmy Carter ever heard of Giovanni Battista Vico, the first modern historian. But it occurs to me that they share his view that decay sets in when societies lose their sense of shame to the point that anything goes.

Jimmy Carter appears to fit the image—or at least comes closest to it among the present crop of politicians—of what the people think is needed. And I think he has a chance of reversing the present depressing moral and political climate if he will pay more attention to the public conscience than to what the self-serving politicians are trying to sell him.

DIFFICULTIES IN THE FIELD OF LAW

Where the law is concerned, it obviously is also in a serious state of dysfunction. It has come to the point where one young lawyer told me a month ago that if he faced a legal problem he could not afford to hire a lawyer. The Chief Justice and others have been issuing warnings to the profession that it is in grave danger—that ways have to be found to curb the truly dreadful amount of litigation. And the average citizen has become contemptuous of the law's so-called "fairness." Some of the rules and regulations have come to be absurd—such as the one that a judge is not permitted to see a defendant's record when assessing whether bail shall be posted.

So many of the things that in years past we saw as fine progressive steps have come to haunt us. We looked on the Legal Aid Societies as voluntary agencies that served the poorer citizens when they needed counsel. Many of us contributed money to maintain these societies. But today we discover that in the major centers Legal Aid has become still another bureaucracy—a system operating under formal grant-aid from cities, states and the national government. The lawyers work under union-type contracts, and the citizen in conflict with the law finds himself up against a new mass of red tape, with a lawyer who has not the slightest interest in the individual, but is concerned only about the extent of plea bargaining and getting rid of another item on the list.

ARROGANCE OF JOURNALISTS

The great moral force of the law needs not to have its batteries recharged; it needs a set of brand-new batteries.

And when we turn our attention to communications, we find the same feelings of distrust. In all the polls taken over the past several years, the American people reveal themselves to regard our communications system as unreliable, and worse, biased.

Years ago, James B. Reston summed up one of the things that has been the curse of journalism for years when he said, "The American newspaperman would rather break a story than understand it." It was true when I was a boy. It is less true today among the better practitioners, but it remains with us like a millstone.

The other millstone we carry to both print and electronic journalism is told in one word: arrogance.

It is the arrogance of not having a decent respect for the immense power we wield—whether it be the printed word or the one broadcast. It is the arrogance of shrugging off complaints and protests about inaccuracies and slanted coverage—the arrogance of printing hurtful half- and quarter-truths on "page one" and relegating weasel-worded corrections to pages 31, 41 or 51. And, worst of all, it is the arrogance of assuming to ourselves the right to criticize everything and everyone in the global society, yet refusing to permit the slightest criticism of journalism.

As with every such truculent statement made, a caveat is in order. Not every journalist, not every newspaper, not every broadcast station is guilty of this indictment. Some are in the forefront of moves for intelligent and responsible change. But there remain too many of the old order—protected in the various ways security blankets are employed—and too many of the young urgently eager to reform the world to their images, but unwilling to tell the essential facts, to make life for journalism difficult.

Yet for all its faults, journalism—indeed, all communications—has to be protected from governmental interference or intrusion or else our society commits intellectual suicide.

This is precisely why The National News Council was brought into being four years ago. It is the largest and most ambitious press council in the world, dwarfing all others by the scope of its reach.

There remains, as might well be expected, some blind and bitter hostility to The News Council within journalism. But the encouraging aspect is that more and more constantly come to recognize that its mission is to serve as the buffer communications needs to protect it from any attempts to impose censorship.

The News Council consists of what we may well term a board of directors—eighteen of them, drawn from both the public and professional sectors. Complaints about inaccuracy or unfairness on the part of news organizations (print or broadcast) are weighed. The Council does not accept complaints about editorial expression or personal opinion, unless facts are in dispute.

The Council has no power to regulate or to impose penalties. It operates openly through public deliberations and the public release of its findings. An Evaluation Committee, set up by the foundations, held that its "importance to the national body politic" was such that it merited all the support it could get. William S. Paley, Chairman of CBS, pledging that network's support, said that The Council

> . . . has reasserted the purpose of the First Amendment by providing a forum through which the American people and their institutions can present their cases when they feel an injustice has been done, without prior restraint being imposed on the news media or retribution being exacted from them. The Council represents a voluntary, noncoercive, affirmative effort, not to impede or to diminish freedom of the press, but to enhance and to elevate it.

SHORTCOMINGS OF LIBRARIANS

Some of you undoubtedly are wondering where the libraries fit into all of this. My placing so much emphasis on the shortcomings of government, the law and the press has been calculating. I submit that many of the same indictments—negativism, absurd internal bureaucratic behavior, arrogance and self-serving interests—apply also to entirely too many in the library field.

It is just as unseemly for those in the library division of communications as it is for those in the related sectors.

The July issue of *Harper's* magazine, just out, carries an article entitled "Busting the Media Trusts." Directed at the now-massive media conglomerates, the article raises the frightening (to me) aspect of an alteration of the First Amendment applications and it describes national unhappiness with the media as having reached the "frenzy" level.

There can be no discussion of the "media" without including the nation's libraries. Obviously, you stand in the front line of those who claim protection of the First Amendment—and deservedly so. Without totally free and complete research information, all of us are lost insofar as reliable checks are concerned.

The central question, it seems to me, is whether all of us at the cutting edge of society have kept our ethical priorities in order—whether in the pursuit of our various duties, we have kept uppermost in mind that we are the servants of the people, and not their masters.

I have been in libraries where the response of those on duty has been quick, interested and extraordinarily helpful. I have been in others where the lack of basic training has been startlingly evident—and in some where the attitudes of those on duty have ranged from open annoyance about being distracted from personal chit-chat to seemingly hostile about the effrontery of anyone daring to ask where certain information may be located.

One has to question the seriousness of purpose of those within libraries who have not had the urge to examine the contents of the great depositories of information gathered in the institutions.

Therefore, I suggest that as you move to consideration of the great needs that confront your libraries, that you not lose sight for one moment of the present deficiencies and faults, such as afflict the other leading agencies in our national society. It calls for an ethical purpose. Without it, you run the risk of the same barrage of criticisms that now descend on government, the law and the press.

You have been studying Daniel Bell's penetrating book, *The Post-Industrial Society.* Kenneth Galbraith has been working along parallel lines and terming it *The New Industrial State.* Both of these distinguished scholars, and others seeking to assess what is developing, are quite right in holding that a major focus for library communications is going to be the professionals—the individuals trained and equipped for the sophisticated judgments needed in directing the new society.

There would, however, come a gross miscarriage of function if the importance all the scholars place on meritocracy is misinterpreted by anyone to equate this vital point with elitism. True, more and more professionals in all the fields will be depending on the library systems for backup and more of everything will be required to service them properly. But this does not mean that your libraries will cease to adequately service those who, for whatever reason, are out of the mainstream. Indeed, this load probably will increase unless there comes a major change in the educational system, and this seems distant at this juncture.

This is the area—dealing with those not in the mainstream—where you may find the tendency toward bureaucratic arrogance hard to contain. But you must contain it or you will help sow the seeds for disaster. No society can tolerate impassively or contemptuously a vast population of the dispossessed. It probably is a fact that library services already are the prime means of reaching those millions who can barely read, or can only grasp information through graphic aids.

USING COMMUNICATION SYSTEMS

Education by video display certainly will become a major issue for librarians. It no longer is simply a national issue. It is global, as you can find out from the current issue of *Atlas World Press Review.* The reports from Britain, France, Venezuela, Japan, Australia, the Soviet Union, and China all tell the same story: concern over the proliferation of entertainment on television. The authoritarian countries have the power to guide this drift to more direct educational information. We are going to have to do it by persuasion, example, and dedicated service.

I discover from *Atlas* the most telling current statistic—that there now are more TV sets in the world than telephones—364 million to 360 million. Obviously, that spread will widen geometrically.

You need no telling that video communication is going to be the standard form of communication for millions in the general public. Some of your libraries are already equipped to some extent in this regard. But what I keep wondering is why the country's libraries seem so inept about communicating what they have to the public.

Almost every agency in national life uses the public service facilities of radio stations and of stores and banks. I go into libraries and occasionally see a bulletin board properly located telling what is new and current and where it can be located. Most of the time, however, I find a vacuum of information about library services. Why, I keep asking myself, do not the libraries avail themselves of the posters that banks and stores are willing to place on display, why the neighborhood newspapers are not given news releases on what the libraries are engaged in currently, why there are no public service announcements on the radio stations? Like other communicators, you have flunked in communicating with the public effectively and consistently.

BECOMING WORKING COMMUNITY CENTERS

All of this suggests that your libraries are going to become working community centers and this will pose some meaningful problems in your staffing. From observation, it has seemed to me that the libraries generally have done better than other agencies in the society in building multi-hued, multi-tongued staffs more representative of our national life.

I would underline this central point by citing the unrest that swept parts of New York's "Spanish Harlem" a few years ago, much of it stemming from the despair of people seeking to deal with the major public hospital in the area. It was one in which the bureaucracy had ignored the need to provide bilingual staffing. People in need of medical service could find no staff members who could speak or understand Spanish. What a farce this was in terms of public service!

We have not before considered this a bilingual nation, but those of us who deal in service and communications are going to have to take into account the self-evident fact that we now have millions of people who cannot read English and who either cannot speak it, or speak it imperfectly. Due to its many-sided problems, the educational institutions, as I indicated earlier, are unlikely to meet this problem quickly and adequately and it may well fall to the libraries to provide the back-up service. If it develops in this manner, you must find ways to teach them our common tongue, and do it with skill and deep understanding.

DEVELOPING A STRONG ETHICAL BASE

Perhaps because of my philosophic stance, I found Professor Bell's *The Cultural Contradictions of Capitalism* a more compelling book than *The Post-Industrial Society.* In it he wrote:

> Any society, in the end, is a moral order that has to justify its principles and the balances of freedoms and coercions. . . . Without a public philosophy explicitly stated, we lack a polity by which we can live by consensus.

In short, you find me once again reaching back to the need for a strong ethical base for all of us in communications.

I commend your president for the bold and imaginative approach to your developing problems. The areas that you will grapple with here—technology, social change, professionalism, economics and public access—are each vital to the society you are serving now and the broader publics you will be serving over this next developing decade.

As you work your way through your various problems and you confront the need for standards—standards that are ever higher—you will find yourself subject to various forms of reasonable argument. Some of it may be what I often call "sweet reason"—the kinds of argument that are marshalled to postpone action until such-and-such steps are taken, or that amount to rationalizations to excuse existing problem situations. Beware of these pressures to move with great caution. Remember Thomas Edison's line that restlessness and discontent are the first necessities of progress.

Or if you wish, accept George Bernard Shaw's definition—that "the reasonable man adapts himself to the world. The unreasonable man persists in trying to adapt the world to himself. Progress, therefore, depends on the unreasonable."

As one whose education has been nurtured out of your stacks of books and the services of your informational services, I have drawn the lessons that nothing in life works without thoughtful purpose, sense of direction, thorough training—and above all, the conviction in and the practice of ethical standards.

Where we have all gone astray in all of the professions has been in abdicating these standards and in being willing to protect selfish interests. Let us, for God's sake, take the high road for a change. So it is that I pray as you move into the details of your work that each of you will keep ever-present the thought that you are toiling in the public interest—public service in its highest form.

For nothing in life is now more important than that the flow of information remain uncontaminated. And, I submit, contamination can come from indecision, from sloth, from carelessness, from a simple lack of ethical purpose.

Cicero said: "To add a library to a house is to give that home a soul." I would like to paraphrase that to have it read:

To have a library system that serves one and all . . . from childhood to old age . . . and at *all* the levels of society . . . is to give a *nation* a soul.

The Impact of Technology on Libraries

by Frederick G. Kilgour

INTRODUCTION

Although the title of this presentation implies that I will be talking mostly about libraries, I wish initially to emphasize that the impact of technology will be largely on people associated with libraries, namely, patrons of libraries and library staff members. To be sure, development of technology will change libraries as institutions, but its most important effect will be perceived by patrons and staff members as individuals.

Except for the introduction into libraries of patron-operated photocopying machines, there has been surprisingly little change in library technology during the past hundred years. Today, however, there is a new kind of technology, the computerized library network, that is changing library staff activities, organization, and procedures. As yet, the computerized library network has had little effect on patrons of libraries, but the next decade will surely witness dramatic improvement in the ability of patrons to obtain needed information from libraries. In general, it can be said that the new technology will be used to promote an evolution in the use of libraries, an evolution of libraries themselves, and an evolution of librarianship.

LIBRARIES CONTAINING ONLY GUTENBERG TECHNOLOGY

I will not attempt to cover every aspect of libraries and their use in this presentation. Therefore, let me review with you a simplified model of a library containing only the products of Gutenberg technology—a simplification in itself. The purpose of a library, as I see it, is to actively participate in the evolution and production of those profoundly human creations: beauty, faith, justice, and knowledge. A library having this purpose can be seen as an organization that intakes, organizes, and lends information. A library must engage in all three of these activities if it is to fulfill its purpose, and the most important of the three is the first, for without intake there would be no library. Next in importance is the central activity—the organization of information—that determines the degree to which a library will fulfill its purpose; this presentation will be devoted to the effect of technology on the organization of information for use.

For an understanding of the relationship to technology of listing, indexing, and classifying information, I will briefly review the history of each topic. The father of modern bibliography, Konrad Gesner, published his *Bibliotheca Universalis* in 1545.[5] Essentially, Gesner undertook a surprisingly successful attempt to list existing books in Greek, Latin, and Hebrew—some twelve thousand items. Gesner hoped that a librarian could use his publication by putting shelf marks beside each title a library possessed, thereby making it unnecessary for each library to catalog an item. His hope is shared by the proponents of present-day computerized library networks.

Gesner entered the titles of books under an author's forename, included an index under surname, and published a score of classified indexes to the main work.

The first published rules for cataloging, only ten in number,[9] were put forth by Thomas Hyde in his preface to the Bodleian catalog published in 1674. Anthony Panizzi published the first cataloging code in English in 1841;[10] Panizzi's ninety-one rules were designed for the construction of the British Museum catalog. In 1852 Charles Coffin Jewett, then at the Smithsonian Institution, published his *On Construction of Catalogues*[7] containing rules based extensively on Panizzi's work and designed to make it possible for catalogers in libraries to produce entries that would be uniform for interfiling into a general catalog. Jewett hoped to develop a technique for maintaining catalog entries on stereotype plates. He planned that a library would send a catalog entry to the Smithsonian, which would convert the entry to a stereotype plate if the collection of plates did not already contain the entry. Jewett proposed to print book form catalogs for libraries by selection of plates from the store, and thereby effect extensive savings in the printing of expensive book form catalogs. Printing of the entire collection of stereotype plates would yield a union catalog.

Charles Ammi Cutter produced the first of four editions of his celebrated *Rules for a Printed Dictionary Catalogue* in 1876;[3] the fourth was published posthumously in 1904. Cutter based his *Rules* to some extent on Jewett's work at mid-century. Subsequent American cataloging codes, beginning with the ALA code in 1908 and including the present *Anglo-American Cataloging Rules* (AACR),[1] have been based on Cutter's work, except that Cutter included rules for subject cataloging whereas American codes subsequent to Cutter have disregarded subject cataloging.

As we have seen, Gesner's scheme for a bibliographic catalog included classified indexes, but it was not until 1843, when Charles Coffin Jewett, then at Brown University, published a structured subject heading index in the Brown University Library catalog[2] that a firm start was made in the alphabetized subject indexing that has become so popular in the United States. The publication of Jewett's subject index marked the beginning of the last great age of librarianship that ended forty years later with Dewey's creation of the full-time reference function in libraries.

In 1848 W. F. Poole, then at Yale University, published his first index to articles in magazines employing the important subject work in the title of the article for subject indexing.[11]

Melvil Dewey initiated an important advance in 1876 with publication of *A Classification and Subject Index for Cataloguing and Arranging the Books and Pamphlets of a Library*[4] that introduced the concept of narrow subject classification for both library catalogs and ordering of books on shelves. In the United States the Dewey classification scheme has been used almost entirely for arrangement of books. Dewey initiated another important advance in facilitating retrieval of subject information from libraries by establishing in 1884 two full-time reference librarians in the Columbia University Library where he was then librarian.

BEGINNINGS OF TECHNOLOGY

The first report on utilization of a computer to retrieve references employing a subject approach was given by Harley E. Tillitt in 1954. Tillitt described information searching using an IBM 701 Calculator at the U.S. Naval Ordinance Test Station, now the Naval Weapons Center, at China Lake, California. The first production of catalog cards by computer was at the Douglas Aircraft Company in 1961.[8]

I will encapsulate the history of technology by emphasizing major developments that have enabled the humanization of human beings. As we all know, primitive man was a food gatherer, and those of us who have seen societies devoted to the gathering of food, such as urban Germany immediately after World War II, know that there is no time or energy available for the creation of beauty, faith, justice, and knowledge.

In the three millennia from 6000 to 3000 B.C. in the Middle East, the food producing revolution occurred wherein humankind settled down to produce food rather than to hunt, and toward the end of that period food production had become so efficient that some members of the community possessed the time and energy to devote themselves to creative enterprises. In the millennium following 3000 B.C. urban society appeared, a result of developments in technology that further freed people from producing food and further enabled individuals to specialize in creation of beauty, faith, justice, and knowledge. Unhappily, the lack of an effective power technology at this time led people to enslave other people as power sources.

Twenty-five centuries later, as western civilization entered the Middle Ages, human muscles were still the major source of power, but during the Middle Ages there occurred a revolution in power that produced such important nonhuman sources of power as the windmill, water mill, horse collar, and fore-and-aft-rigged ship. As western civilization evolved out of the Middle Ages, it was no longer solely dependent on human sources of power for it had efficient, nonhuman sources. People began to control production and use of power rather than produce it themselves; hence, the productivity of individuals rapidly increased.

The industrial revolution of the eighteenth and nineteenth centuries, with its invention of the steam engine whose location was not limited to stream side or a windy plain, and its development of the machine tool relieving people of laborious manual tasks, further enhanced human productivity. People increasingly became learners as well as workers, as the development of mechanics' libraries in the early nineteenth century testifies.

Until the middle of the nineteenth century the development of technology had been almost entirely a series of cut-and-dry events. After this time, an ever-increasing body of scientific knowledge enabled the application of science to technological goals.

THE DIGITAL COMPUTER AND LIBRARIES

By the mid-twentieth century, developments in electrical technology enabled the invention of the digital computer, an extremely rapid information processing machine, which has relieved hordes of people from simple, repetitive, clerical-like activities. The computer has accelerated development of the post-industrial, information-based society of today, and electronic information processing in libraries, although in its infancy, has already relieved some groups of staff members of simple, repetitive dehumanizing tasks and begun an increase in staff productivity.

Let us now relate computer technology to the organization of information in libraries for use. Descriptive cataloging is, as we all know, controlled by cataloging codes, and the better the code the less opportunity for human judgment. As Jewett put it in an oft-quoted statement:

> The rules for cataloguing must be stringent, and should meet as far as possible all difficulties of detail. Nothing, so far as can be avoided, should be left to the individual taste or judgment of the cataloguer.[6]

Humanization of descriptive cataloging obviously requires the discard of "stringent" rules, depriving people of judgment, such as we now have in four hundred pages of AACR. Such rules are required, however, for the construction of alphabetical catalogs and in particular for alphabetical union catalogs, where uniformity of entry is absolutely imperative. The catalogs that Jewett intended to produce were printed book form catalogs. For the union card catalogs of a century later, it was even more imperative that entries should be uniform, since in a card catalog only one entry can be seen at a time whereas in a book catalog perhaps as many as fifty can be viewed at once. As we have seen, Gesner's catalog and every alphabetical catalog since Gesner has consisted of a linear arrangement of entries. Clearly, some other catalog design is required if we are to move on from the mechanical application of detailed rules.

Computer technology has already provided us with a new design for library catalogs that will obviate use of detailed rules. Several large on-line computerized catalogs do not consist of a linear arrangement of entries as is the case in alphabetical card and printed catalogs. Rather, these catalogs consist of a myriad of miniature catalogs. The Ohio College Library Center's on-line catalog containing over three million entries actually consists of over two and a half million of these miniature catalogs. No miniature catalog in the OCLC system, as presented to a user, contains more than 250 entries, and only a few percent contain more than thirty-two entries. It is obvious that in a cataloging system where the catalogs never contain more than 250 entries, detailed rules such as those in AACR are unnecessary. Therefore, we can expect in the near future a mechanized, and hopefully a computerized, type of cataloging employing only information on title pages, with the addition of cross-references. Hopefully, the edition of AACR currently being reworked will be the last of the detailed cataloging codes.

Experimentation on computerization of subject indexing and classification has been carried out at various research centers, but as yet there is no extensive application of the knowledge coming out of these experiments. Applications have lagged because methods used in the experiments would be cumbersome and costly in application. Nevertheless, we can anticipate that the years ahead will bring economic computerization of indexing and classification.

In the long run the computerization of cataloging that will increase productivity of staff will undoubtedly be beneficial to individual staff members, but in the short run can be harmful. Those libraries effectively using the shared cataloging systems of computerized networks are able to reduce the number of staff members involved in cataloging. In many libraries this reduction has been achieved by normal attrition, but there certainly have been cases where people have been terminated because they were no longer needed. As advantage is taken in the future of the new design of on-line catalogs, there will be extensive reduction in cataloging staffs. As yet the profession has done no planning to relieve the harmful impact on individuals of technological unemployment; such planning should be undertaken now to minimize possible harmful effects on individual staff members. If we wait until the crisis is upon us, some of our colleagues will be unnecessarily harmed.

The long-range, beneficial effects of computerization of cataloging will include, of course, an improved economic status for libraries and librarians, but perhaps more important is the fact that computerization is opening up new areas for intellectual activity. During the past hundred years librarians have been singularly devoid of fruitful professional ideas in contrast to artists, jurists, scientists, physicians, and engineers. Just as important scientific concepts open up new areas for investigation, so does computerization open up new areas in librarianship for research and development.

Improvement in the availability of library resources for library patrons has already begun to occur. Some computerized library networks automatically build an on-line union catalog as participants utilize shared cataloging processes. Perhaps the most dramatic development to date has been the increased availability of resources in smaller libraries, many of which now send out interlibrary loans in response to requests they never received before participation in an on-line union catalog.

As most of you know, there are many large databases available containing indexing of articles in journals, magazines, and newspapers, as well as indexing of reports, but as yet there is no analogous subject retrieval available for large on-line monograph catalogs except for the BALLOTS system, which requires use of the exact subject heading for retrieval. Experimental development of subject retrieval from large on-line files is currently underway, and its successful application will measurably increase success of library patrons in finding information they require.

IMPACT OF COMPUTER TECHNOLOGY

The principal impact of computer technology on libraries has been improvement in economic status of libraries and enhancement of resource sharing among libraries. Economic improvement has come from computerized library networks making available mechanized processes as well as economies of scale. Over ninety percent of the cataloging by participants in the OCLC system utilizes catalog records already in the system. As computerized library networks continue to make it possible for libraries to lower the rate of rise of their per-unit costs, libraries will experience an increasingly firm economic base, thereby enabling libraries and librarianship to move into a future brighter than the immediate past.

Resource sharing among libraries is not new, but broadly effective resource sharing among libraries is new and has been made possible by computerized library networks. This broad sharing of resources has invalidated the pyramidal concept of a national library, for it is now clear, as I have said before, that the national library is the nation's libraries. Every library participating in a computerized network makes location information about its resources almost instantly available, and it is turning out that the magnitude of these resources is far greater than anyone expected. Intelligent use of knowledge of resources is beginning to enable libraries to improve the effectiveness of their expenditures for acquisitions by eliminating duplication of little used materials among neighborly institutions, and further improvement can be expected in the future.

SUMMARY AND CONCLUSIONS

In summary, we can say that technology will reduce the number of positions of certain types, but in the long run will provide more jobs associated with new developments. At the same time the new positions will bring with them heightened intellectual activities and challenges, and in this sense will increase the humanization of librarianship.

As for library patrons, they will experience a higher percentage of successes in obtaining information from libraries, and will be better informed as required in an information-based society. As for libraries, they will more actively participate in production and evolution of beauty, faith, justice, and knowledge, and on an increasingly firm economic base. It is appropriate to end with a concluding paragraph of the philosopher Alfred North Whitehead's Lowell Lectures in 1925:

> Modern science has imposed on humanity the necessity for wandering. Its progressive thought and its progressive technology make the transition through time, from generation to generation, a true migration into uncharted seas of adventure. The very benefit of wandering is that it is dangerous and needs skill to avert evils. We must expect, therefore, that the future will disclose dangers. It is the business of the future to be dangerous; and it is among the merits of science that it equips the future for its duties. The prosperous middle classes, who ruled the nineteenth century, placed an excessive value upon placidity of existence. They refused to face the necessities for social reform imposed by the new industrial system, and they are now refusing to face the necessities for intellectual reform imposed by the new knowledge. The middle class pessimism over the future of the world comes from a confusion between civilization and security. In the immediate future there will be less security than in the immediate past, less stability. It must be admitted that there is a degree of instability which is inconsistent with civilization. But, on the whole, the great ages have been unstable ages.[12]

Technology is moving librarianship into another of its great ages.

REFERENCES

1. *Anglo-American Cataloging Rules.* Chicago: American Library Association, 1967.
2. *A Catalogue of the Library . . . with an Index of Subjects.* Providence, RI: Brown University Library, 1843.
3. Cutter, Charles A. *Rules for a Printed Dictionary Catalogue.* Washington, DC: Government Printing Office, 1876.
4. Dewey, Melvil. *A Classification and Subject Index for Cataloguing and Arranging the Books and Pamphlets of a Library.* Amherst, MA: 1876.

5. Gesner, Konrad. *Bibliotheca Universalis.* Zurich: C. Froschauer, 1545.
6. Harris, Michael H., ed. *The Age of Jewett; Charles Coffin Jewett and American Librarianship, 1841-1868.* Littleton, CO: Libraries Unlimited, 1975. p. 101.
7. Jewett, Charles C. *On the Construction of Catalogues of Libraries and Their Publication by Means of Separate, Stereotyped Titles.* Washington, DC: Smithsonian Institution, 1852.
8. Kilgour, Frederick G. "History of Library Computerization," *Journal of Library Automation* 3:218-29 (September 1970).
9. Norris, Dorothy M. *A History of Cataloguing and Cataloguing Methods 1100-1850.* London: Grafton, 1939. pp. 151-2.
10. Panizzi, Anthony. "Rules for the Compilation of the Catalogue," *Catalogue of Printed Books in the British Museum.* London: British Museum, Dept. of Printed Books, 1841. pp. v-ix.
11. Poole, William F. *An Alphabetical Index to Subjects, Treated in the Reviews, and Other Periodicals.* New York: Putnam, 1848.
12. Whitehead, Alfred North. *Science and the Modern World.* New York: Macmillan, 1931. pp. 298-9.

The Impact of Technology on Libraries and Librarians: A Literature Review

by Susan K. Martin

Technological developments in the broadest sense have been incorporated in libraries since the first formal library. From the stylus and papyrus to ballpoint pens, typewriters, and telephones, the pace of technology has been felt by the information profession. For the purposes of this discussion, however, "technology" will be limited to the significant tools of this century: computers, educational technology, television and telecommunications.

A noticeable characteristic of the "impact of technology on libraries" is that few writers have addressed that subject directly. Much has been published about specific applications of technology, either within particular institutions or within the profession as a whole. "How we did it good" literature abounds. It is possible to extract from this professional literature a picture of the impact of technology to date, and also to obtain a glimpse of possible future impact. However, straightforward discussion of the topic is rare. Why? Perhaps we are unwilling to examine carefully the results of our decisions and actions, or perhaps the topic is at once too enormous and too dynamic to be addressed cogently by a single author.

Among those who have examined the forces of technology and libraries is Vagianos,[33] who points out that new technologies, rather than representing a revolutionary process, are merely logical evolutions of the past and the present. They ". . . do not provide totally new services; they inevitably increase costs . . .; and they often impede service because they require social engineering to reduce their institutional drawbacks." The problem of institutional impediments is addressed in detail by Veaner,[34] who suggests that technology must be used to solve the library's organizational problems. Dillon[8] identified the separation between documents, databases, and data as a flow in our information systems which could be overcome with integrated systems such as the one proposed by Project INTREX.[29] In discussing library uses of technology, Fussler[12] and Kilgour[17] predicted long-range institutional and service gains.

In 1977, library technology is being brought to bear on the goal of a national bibliographic network, proposed and outlined by the National Commission on Libraries and Information Science.[25] With the experience from several regional networks, libraries are now better able to conceive of a network which would link the resources of the entire country. Livingston[20] predicts a network of between two and nine "nodes." Reynolds[31] states that communication within the involved organizations, education of nonlibrarians and adept library administration will be necessary to pave the way for successful networks.

APPLICATIONS: TECHNICAL AND PUBLIC SERVICES

Following a few years of initiation and learning, librarians are easily working with computer terminals, microforms, and other technological wonders. In a nationwide survey, Bierman[3] reported that a sizable number of libraries are either using book or microform catalogs or plan to do so in the near future. On-line replacement of the catalog appears, however, to be considered economically unfeasible. From a library experience with the Ohio College Library Center (OCLC) system, Ohmes and Jones[28] describe the advantages and disadvantages of using an on-line system for processing. With similar experience, Nitecki[27] presents tables of costs and productivity for manual and on-line cataloging which indicate that, although the system was not without problems, the additional productivity gained by using OCLC was well worth the investment. Baldwin[2] shows that the manner in which a library approaches technological change has a vast impact on the success and cost-effectiveness of the system.

Suddenly, on-line reference services are receiving considerable attention. Because the commercial services are relatively easy to obtain, many libraries wish to provide the extended search capability. However, because the services are not inexpensive, libraries are struggling with the question of charging their patrons for these services. Gardner and Wax[13] claim that libraries will be unable to provide the service without charge, and that strategies for implementation of the services will have to change in order to achieve user acceptance. With this claim, they reinforce an opinion expressed by De Gennaro,[7] that reference librarians will become intermediaries as libraries become brokers for on-line services from vendors. Based on a survey of members of the Reference and Adult Services Division, Nitecki[26] shows that while the majority of reference librarians feel that on-line services should be made available to their patrons, extra funding will be required.

Circulation systems, the grandfather of automated library applications, are continuing to undergo change and development. McGee,[24] Foil and Carter,[11] and Burgess[6] discuss the equipment used for circulation systems and the cost-effectiveness of the systems.

TOOLS: MICROFORM, VIDEO AND CABLE, AUDIOVISUAL, MINICOMPUTERS

In a recent review of micrographics literature, Spigai and Butler[32] assert that "microform has almost disappeared"—that microforms are being accepted and integrated into information systems, rather than being held aside. Malinconico[21] describes the advantages of Computer Output Microform (COM) catalogs, comparing them with on-line and book catalogs. With incisive questions about the validity of retaining card catalogs, Elrod[10] reports the creation, maintenance, and justification for a COM catalog at the University of British Columbia.

As Marquis[22] suggests in the Prologue, we are moving from a distributive and material-oriented society to an information-oriented one. Brong[5] describes developments in telecommunications, and claims that without adequate retraining, personnel may be "the weakest link in the total library/information system." Recent efforts have increased the involvement of librarians in video and cable activities; Kenney[16] and Lacomb[18] summarize legislative barriers and describe existing and planned activities of libraries and information centers. For video and cable, as for audiovisual activities, sections have been formed within the Information Science and Automation Division to provide a membership base for librarians working with education technology.

The uncertainty of librarians and libraries toward audiovisual materials is aptly portrayed by Boyle.[4] AV services are beginning to expand, but our minds still place the materials and services *outside* the library's collections, just as microforms once were. Lieberman[19] argues that audiovisual services are in fact an integral part of library services and should be thus regarded.

Minicomputers developed and proliferated so rapidly that microcomputers were available almost before any written documentation had appeared on the use of the minicomputer. For example, Pearson[30] reviews the literature on minicomputers in libraries, and relies heavily on data processing publications as his sources. We may never see a large amount of publishing on minicomputers, because their applications in libraries are not very different from our experiences with large-scale computers five and ten years ago. Grosch[14] describes minicomputer requirements and the design of a library management application at the University of Minnesota.

Services provided by commercial firms are, more and more, based on the same technological uses as those employed in libraries. This writer[23] evaluates the role of vendors in library services and systems, library-oriented hardware, and telecommunications.

STAFF

In the area of the impact of technology on staff, the profession again appears to be hiding from reality. Impacts will be felt, and librarians must be prepared for them. Dougherty[9] predicts that new technologies will force us to rethink our organizations and services; staff will have to be retrained and reallocated so that the library can deal successfully with the changing environment. From a library already familiar with technological change, Horny[15] stresses the need for communication and the potential impact of reorganization. Atherton[1] reiterates these points:

> . . . the evolutionary extensions of the traditional bound-volume library brought about by technological innovations must be properly assessed by the top managers of these libraries with an eye to accommodating these changes in personnel, and they must plan to revise the . . . objectives of the libraries.

Librarians, then, must be willing to examine the impact of technology on their institutions. In an age of accountability, we will find that if we do not take responsibility for these changes, our governing authorities will. We must also be aware of the effect of general economic conditions, realizing that we probably would not cooperate, would not give up our parallel and duplicate systems, if we had the wherewithal to remain independent. The changing economy and the developing technology move hand in hand to provide an environment for resource-sharing and nationwide accessibility to information. Libraries and librarians are in an admirable position to take advantage of these increasingly sophisticated technologies.

REFERENCES

1. Atherton, Pauline. "Systems Personnel: What Are Our Needs?" *Library Automation: The State of the Art II.* Susan K. Martin and Brett Butler, eds. Chicago: American Library Association, 1975.
2. Baldwin, Paul E. *Bibliographic Control Problems and Organizational Charge Issues Posed by the Implementation of a Computer-Based Cooperative Cataloging Support System.* Burnaby, BC: Simon Fraser University, 1976. Master's thesis.
3. Bierman, Kenneth J. "Automated Alternatives to Card Catalogs: The Current State of Planning and Implementation," *Journal of Library Automation* 8:277-98. (December 1975).
4. Boyle, Deirdre. "Libraries and Media," *Library Journal* 101: 125-29. (January 1, 1976).
5. Brong, Gerald R. "The Technologies of Education and Communication," *Advances in Librarianship.* Vol. 5, Melvin J. Voigt ed. New York: Academic Press, 1975.
6. Burgess, Thomas K. "A Cost Effectiveness Model for Comparing Various Circulation Systems," *Journal of Library Automation* 6:75-86. (June 1973).
7. De Gennaro, Richard. "Providing Bibliographic Services From Machine-Readable Data Bases—The Library's Role," *Journal of Library Automation* 6:215-22. (December 1973).

8. Dillon, Martin. "The Impact of Automation on the Content of Libraries and Information Centers," *College and Research Libraries* 34:418-25. (November 1973).
9. Dougherty, Richard M. "The Impact of Networks on Library Operations," presented at ASIA Annual Meeting. San Francisco, 1976.
10. Elrod, McRee J. "Is the Card Catalogue's Unquestioned Sway in North America Ending?" *Journal of Academic Librarianship* 2:4-8. (March 1976).
11. Foil, Patti Sue and Bradley D. Carter. "Survey of Data Collection Systems for Computer Based Library Circulation Processes," *Journal of Library Automation* 9:222-33. (September 1976).
12. Fussler, Herman. *Research Libraries and Technology.* Report of the Sloan Foundation. Chicago: University of Chicago Press, 1973.
13. Gardner, Jeffrey J. and David M. Wax. "Online Bibliographic Services," *Library Journal* 101:1827-32. (September 15, 1976).
14. Grosch, Audrey N. "Mini-computers for Library Management Application: A New Approach to Bibliographic Processing," *Computers in Information Data Centers.* Joe Ann Clifton and Duane Helgeson eds. Montvale, NJ: AFIPS Press, 1973.
15. Horny, Karen. "Automation of Technical Services: Northwestern's Experience," *College and Research Libraries* 35:364-69. (September 1974).
16. Kenney, Brigitte L. "The Future of Cable Communications in Libraries," *Journal of Library Automation* 9:299-317. (December 1976).
17. Kilgour, Frederick G. "Evolving, Computerizing, Personalizing," *American Libraries* 3:141-47. (February 1972).
18. Lacomb, Denis J. "Video Technology," *Library Journal* 101:2003-9. (October 1, 1976).
19. Lieberman, Irving. "Audiovisual Services in Libraries," *Annual Review of Information Science and Technology.* Vol. 5, Melvin J. Voigt, ed. New York: Academic Press, 1975.
20. Livingston, Lawrence G. "Advisory Group on National Bibliographic Control," in Association of Research Libraries. *Minutes of the 88th Meeting, May 6-7, 1976, Seattle, Washington.* Washington, DC: ARL, 1976.
21. Malinconico, S. Michael. "The Display Medium and the Price of the Message," *Library Journal* 101:2144-50. (October 15, 1976).
22. Marquis, Rollin. "Post-Industrial Society and the Growth of Information: The Impact on Libraries," *The Information Society: Issues and Answers.* E. J. Josey, ed. Phoenix, AZ: The Oryx Press, 1978.

23. Martin, Susan K. *Library Networks, 1976-77.* White Plains, NY: Knowledge Industry Publications, 1976.
24. McGee, Rob S. "The University of Chicago Library's JRL 100 Circulation Terminal and Bar-Coded Labels," *Journal of Library Automation* 8:5-25. (March 1975).
25. National Commission on Libraries and Information Science. *A National Program for Library and Information Services.* Washington, DC: NCLIS, 1975.
26. Nitecki, Danuta A. "Attitudes Toward Automated Information Retrieval Services Among RASD Members," *RQ* 16:133-41. (Winter 1976).
27. Nitecki, Joseph Z. *OCLC in Retrospect: A Review of the Impact of the OCLC on the Administration of a Large University Technical Services Operation.* Philadelphia: Temple University, January 1974. ED 087 482.
28. Ohmes, Frances and J. F. Jones. "The Other Half of Cataloging," *Library Resources Technical Services* 17:320-29. (Summer 1973).
29. Overhage, Carl F. J. and Joyce R. Harman, eds. Planning Conference on Information Transfer Experiments (INTREX), Woods Hole, MA, 2 August - 3 September 1965. *Report* Cambridge, MA: M.I.T. Press, 1965.
30. Pearson, Karl M. Jr. "Minicomputers in the Library," *Annual Review of Information Science and Technology.* Vol. 10, Carlos A. Cuadra, ed. Washington DC: American Society for Information Science, 1975.
31. Reynolds, Maryan E. "Challenges of Modern Network Development," *Journal of Academic Librarianship* 1:19-22. (May 1975).
32. Spigai, Frances G. and Brett Butler. "Micrographics," *Annual Review of Information Science and Technology.* Vol. 11, Margha Williams, ed. Washington, DC: American Society for Information Science, 1976.
33. Vagianos, Louis. "Today IS Tomorrrow: A Look at the Future Information Arena," *Library Journal* 101:147-56. (January 1, 1976).
34. Veaner, Allen B. "Institutional Political and Fiscal Factors in the Development of Library Automation, 1967-71," *Journal of Library Automation* 7:5-26. (March 1974).

The Impact of Social Change on Libraries

by Major Owens

INTRODUCTION

Within the past fifteen years we have experienced a number of crises which are reflective of the kind of social change pressing ceaselessly upon our society. In a brief span of time we have been confronted with the civil rights crisis; the Viet Nam War crisis; the environmental dangers crisis; the energy crisis; and a continuing crisis of economic uncertainty. Closely related to these crises are certain social phenomena and certain mass behavior patterns which are sometimes the result of social change and sometimes the cause of change. The sweeping demographic upheavals within our inner cities; the increasing number of persons utilizing complex government assistance programs; the mounting pressure for more citizen participation in institutional and governmental decision-making; the increasing use of litigation and the systematic group approach to advocacy; and the continuing and intensifying demand for various forms of nonformal education; these are examples of such phenomena and patterns.

The conclusion reached by Rollin Marquis in the Prologue for this symposium provides a good summary for part of what I am trying to describe:

> Resistance to bureaucracy, claiming of social rights, determination of social policy, demands for social and economic benefits may increasingly be effected by collective negotiation or action through participatory citizen movements, communities of interest, pressure groupings of the class action and advocacy type.

As these currents of change race along, where are the librarians? Where were they yesterday? Where are they today? Where are they likely to be in the future? Will they be on the shore watching the currents sweep along or will they be getting wet in some significant place out there in the stream?

At this point in the history of the profession, this question is still very much an open one. The very thorough and impressive literature review by Leigh Estabrook and Thomas Blumenthal confirms the fact that: ". . . while the problem was most frequently debated in the late

1960s and early '70s, it remains unresolved." Our task here is not to discuss the positions we should take and the actions we should join as individual citizens of local communities and the nation. Our task here is to discuss the special reactions to social change needed from librarians. As society at large struggles to cope with social change, what is the unique contribution librarians *qua* librarians have to make?

Since it appears that the conclusion of the literature search has unearthed very little evidence of a positive impact of social change on the library, perhaps insight may be gained by approaching the problem from another direction. Let us explore for a moment the negative impact of social change.

THE NEGATIVE IMPACT OF SOCIAL CHANGE: FAILURES TO RESPOND

Within the profession and the related organizations and institutions, for every major social change, somewhere there will be found an example of an imaginative and magnificent response. There is no phenomenon which has not, in some isolated instance, received a reaction from an institution or individual librarian. The problem, however—and the only discussion worthy of this forum—is the problem of the collective response, the volume of response. In other words when you weigh the number of responses to social change against the great volume of people, organizations and activities which make up the library profession and the library world, the responses have generally been insignificant. When one examines the monstrous dimensions of social change within our society and compares this phenomenon to the microscopic reactions within our library world, one may reasonably conclude that we have not permitted social change to have any basic impact upon us.

There have not been enough worthy reactions rising to meet the challenges thrown at our feet; we have refused to acknowledge the seriousness of critical situations and pressures. Of course, if we accept the argument that inaction and passivity are a form of response, then the record will show that we have responded. We have scampered fearfully out of the path of oncoming dislocations and upheavals, government policies threatening world peace, mass institutional denials of human rights, recessions and budget cuts; and we have retreated, acquiesced and adjusted. This kind of impact can be measured negatively. In descriptive and qualitative terms, such negative impact may be documented by listing our failures and reviewing our sins of omission. The refusal to encourage citizen participation, the unwillingness to campaign for increased budget allocations, the resolutions not proposed, the policies not promulgated, the LSCA grants consumed but denied the chance to change "regular" library functions and procedures, the library school courses not offered, undrafted standards, undrafted legislation, experiments never conceptualized, techniques never tested; these and numerous similar items combine to fill up a great hole of nothingness, a dangerous void, a bottomless pit on the social landscape.

Our great crime of omission is that we have allowed a vacuum to develop and expand within our complex society. The things we have not done, the failures of librarians, have fostered a great social undernourishment and malnourishment. As time has woven an increasingly complex social fabric, certain threads and strands were left out because librarians did not step forward to weave in that portion and those materials that only the library profession could know were needed and only librarians knew how to include.

Please pardon the heavy use of figures of speech in these introductory remarks. For the rest of this presentation I will focus on specifics and deal with details. The following are a few examples of our failure to respond adequately:

I. We have failed to clarify and update the goals, role and function of the library profession in the evolving society.

II. There has been a failure of administrative imagination. We have not expanded and updated traditional concepts and systems to absorb new functions. We have not remodeled existing basic systems.

III. We have failed to duplicate and replicate the best models and experiments and to interject successful new ideas and approaches into the mainstream of institutional operations. And closely related is the failure to interject new ideas into the professional education process.

Since these three failures are closely related, let us elaborate on them jointly. These three failures appear to also be concerns of the Advisory Committee of the White House Conference on Libraries. Eight program objectives are listed in the minutes of the first meeting of the Advisory Committee. Among these eight, the following are addressed to the first three failures enumerated above:

(1) Ensure that basic minimums of library and information services adequate to meet the needs of all local communities are satisfied.

(2) Provide adequate special services to special constituencies including the unserved.

(3) Strengthen existing statewide resources and systems.

(4) Coordinate existing Federal programs of library and information services.

(5) Ensure basic and continuing education.

In order to reach the objectives of assuring that basic minimums are satisfied and providing special services to special constituencies we must first achieve clarity with respect to such functions as outreach, information and referral, advocacy and a few others. There is general agreement within the profession on the role of the library as a storehouse for knowledge; however, at this late date there is still confusion with respect to the information dissemination function. Does ALA presently have or is it preparing minimum standards for outreach services and for information and referral services? Can we respond to the sweeping demographic changes within our inner cities if we do not assign priority to these two activities.

Related to this failure to clarify goals is the failure of administrative imagination. More imagination would allow library bureaucrats to perceive that certain traditional functions are not so far removed from the new services being demanded. Information and referral services may be developed as an expansion of traditional reference service. Detroit's TIP (The Information Place) program is not an experimental appendage attached to regular library services. TIP is at the heart of the total service program and it is the creation of librarians. Advocacy counseling for individuals or for groups may be developed as an extension of the reader's advisor concept. In order to respond to the needs of the increased number of persons utilizing complex government assistance programs, and in order to provide information for the lay advocacy and citizen lobbying groups, we must use our imagination to stretch the traditional services.

The third failure is, of course, closely related to the first two, and this focuses on our failure to duplicate and replicate the best models and experiments. Let me repeat an earlier statement: Within the profession, for every major social change, somewhere there will be found an example of an imaginative and magnificent response. But a few successful neighborhood information center programs like the Houston Public Library program are not enough. A few community coordinators, job information centers, and media mobiles cannot meet the need. The media equipment and arrangements of the Hennepin County Library and the model of basic services of the Nassau Public Library represent implementations of visions of the future. All of these models must become routine and commonplace. The duty of the profession is to guarantee a process which more rapidly absorbs, duplicates, and replicates the best of what blossoms forth to meet needs. And in this process library schools must play a major role.

But let me move to failure number four, for here I'm certain to arouse some excitement:

> IV. We have failed to carry our intellectual freedom responsibilities and policies to their logical conclusion.

With respect to this failure I do not wish to cite any of the related program objectives of the Advisory Committee of the White House Conference. Instead I suggest we closely examine the implications of the overall theme of the White House Conference: "Equal Opportunity of Access." My contention here is that the ALA Intellectual Freedom Committee should have long ago become the "Equal Opportunity of Access" Committee. The right to read, to hear, to view, is a hallowed right if there is no access. The great tragedy of the ALA encounter with the Viet Nam monstrosity is that action came so late and it was not advanced as an intellectual freedom concern. The cover up at Mai Lai, the distortions of the daily war news, the Pentagon Papers; these are a few of the items related to that holocaust which required commentary and action by librarians in their professional capacity as librarians. It is also regrettable that our profession has not played a more central role in the push for sunshine laws and freedom of information laws. Even the continuing question related to pornography and community moral standards acquires a new lustre when you ponder the right of every citizen to have access to the documents and exhibits used by judges and other public officials in reaching their determinations with respect to community moral standards; and the right of these same citizens to demand that the public library serve as the instrument which provides access to these public documents.

The fifth and final failure:

V. We have failed to achieve a minimum mastery of the political and public policy-making process.

Related to this failure you will find among the White House Conference program objectives, the following:

(1) Establish a locus of federal responsibility charged with implementing the national network and coordinating the National Program under the policy guidance of the National Commission.

(2) Plan, develop and implement a nationwide network of library and information service.

(3) Encourage the private sector (comprising organizations which are not directly tax supported) to become an active partner in the development of the National Program.

In a period of great preoccupation with balanced budgets and reductions in government spending, these objectives cannot be accomplished without great public support. In the past we have shown little concern for the political process; to achieve public support at the local, state and national level, minimum competence in the art of influencing and pressuring must be achieved.

STRATEGIES TO OVERCOME FAILURES

The instructions for this forum stated that I must react to the issues, clarify and define the critical questions, and project into the future. To each of the failures I have briefly cited, at this point, I would like to be able to project into the immediate future a strategy for overcoming that failure. Unfortunately, limitations on time will not permit a detailed discussion of a strategy for each failure. Given the circumstances, I propose to lay out a blueprint for overcoming that failure which I consider the most devastating: the failure to achieve a minimum mastery of the political and public policy-making process.

But before I begin let me state emphatically that there is one activity which must be a cornerstone for all five strategies. The White House Conference on Libraries presents us with a golden opportunity which must not be squandered. For the next twenty to twenty-four months we have a vehicle, a gimmick, to capture the attention of the American public. As we move progressively closer to the conference, the media will inevitably become more accessible. To take full advantage of this spotlight focused on the profession, let us today declare a state of emergency. It is necessary to place the profession on a war footing and demand of ourselves a superhuman effort during this period. We cannot solve every problem and overcome all failures but it is possible to set in motion a momentum that will sweep us to new levels. It is possible to create the public consciousness which is vital. It is possible to lock in the major decision-makers at a level of commitment which will provide the resources to realize a new age of library and information services. If we set up the scenario with energy and imagination, all of this and more can be delivered by the White House Conference.

Specifically, in the area of political action our strategy must begin with the launching of a drive to maximize—between now and the end of the White House Conference—the number and the scope of legislative proposals at the federal and state level. The call should go out immediately to every state library association; deadlines for responses should be set; guidelines to guarantee that important options are considered must be issued. In addition to content and substance this crash mobilization must be concerned with process. The general public and other professionals must be encouraged to participate in the development of new legislation. We should take this opportunity to practice ways to overcome one element of the failure of the profession in the political arena, and that is the failure to allow citizen participation in policy decision-making. The following represents some of the steps which must be taken in order to conduct an effective legislative "blitz" at the state and local level:

1. Strengthen and broaden the participation in the professional groups responsible for legislation—library association committees, trustee committees, governors' commissions, etc.

2. Complete an analysis of the governance and funding situation. Does the state constitution require that libraries be established and maintained? Can references to education in the state constitution be interpreted to include library services? Are there other statutes or charters where library funding is mandated as an ongoing obligation?

3. Examine optional models and choose one or a combination as the basis for a legislative proposal on governance and permanent funding. This must be at the core of most legislative packages.
4. Priorities for additional legislative proposals must be set in accordance with the situation of social change within the state. If for example, there is a great demand for various forms of nonformal education, then priority must go to legislation designed to provide libraries with resources to assist in meeting this need.
5. All state legislative efforts must include legislation which enables the state to establish linkages with the projected national network and enables the state to qualify for matching funds and other benefits.

After the legislative package is completed it is then necessary to develop strategies for obtaining passage:

6. The proposals must be widely distributed with maximum publicity and an invitation to the broadest possible cross section of citizens. Ways must be found to systematically obtain feedback and to respond to expressed public concerns.
7. A listing of organizational allies must be completed and a conscious effort must be made to obtain their active involvement in the campaign to achieve passage of the legislation. Allies from the business community are of vital importance and their participation will be more intense if there are specific proposals included which relate to business and industry. Environment protection groups, consumer advocates, the good government groups which promoted the freedom of information laws; these and other similar activists are also possible staunch allies.
8. A core of legislators who will serve as sponsors must be cultivated. Since only governors have the authority to convene state conferences as prerequisites to the White House Conference, special efforts must be made to win the enthusiastic support of chief state executives.
9. An organized brigade of librarians and other interested citizens must be developed and maintained to assist the legislative sponsors in marshalling whatever resources and pressures are needed. Citizen lobbying is an art being practiced effectively by many other groups with less talent than the library profession.

By June of 1978, an omnibus legislative package should be in motion within every state. The proposals should address themselves to every problem and deficiency which legislation can possibly cure.

Utilizing such a comprehensive approach, we should not be discouraged when there are casualties; some proposals will be rejected immediately and some will be amended beyond recognition. We should also not be naive and assume that there is only a world of friends and supporters waiting for us. Libraries have enemies and any effort to make the profession more effective in the process of social change will generate more enemies. Serious legislative campaigns may create controversy—especially where constitutional amendments are proposed to mandate permanent funding for libraries. And let us not forget the enemy within, the tenacious fifth column of librarians who insist that concern with social change is not a part of our job description; those who are monumentally stupid enough to think that we should not seek more state and federal support; those who believe that libraries can be preserved as low energy activities and perpetually quiet places; those combinations of the dodo bird and ostrich are still powerful forces to be reckoned with. Remember that we are in a state of emergency; we should not shrink from intellectual combat and we should not hesitate to throw some adversaries up against the wall. Figuratively speaking, it is our duty to liberate the profession from their poisonous influences.

Assuming that we shall overcome the saboteurs and those sincere colleagues who just don't have any vision, we should emerge from the state battlegrounds with enough victories to provide great impetus for solidifying proposals for national legislation. The results of the people's deliberations within the states should be combined with the expertly designed proposals of the National Commission. One cannot predict the details of the final consensus package. In my opinion we can claim victory with honor if the legislative package which is finalized at the White House Conference and later passed by Congress establishes the following principles:

1. That library and information services are vitally necessary for the survival of our complex American democracy and therefore the provision of such services as an ongoing and permanent obligation must be authorized and mandated by law. Libraries cannot survive if they continue to be subject to the whims of annual budget makers. Conditions placed on federal aid may partially achieve such state and local legal mandates.

2. That every government program, agency or activity must provide funding, as a percentage of its overall budget, for the dissemination of information. To give the "Equal Opportunity of Access" theme real meaning and to make the freedom of information laws functional, adequate financing of the information effort must be made available. At least seventy-five percent of such funds should be allocated to public, academic, school and special libraries. Citizens at every

level are increasingly more involved with their government and this provision represents a practical approach toward meeting their need to know.

3. That the federal government must serve as the prime mover and provide the capital funding for a national information network. Other publicly funded databases such as the space information center, the Bureau of the Census and the unclassified material of the Central Intelligence Agency should be made an integral part of the network. Where fees must be charged for machine searches, the principle of "lifeline" rates must be utilized.

4. That there should be "federal certification" of the nonfederal databases to be included in the national network. While local communities and libraries may retain the power to choose their own areas of specialization, the inclusion of a collection or database in the network should be dependent on such elements as extent of coverage, capacity for growth, agency administrative capacity, consistency, quality control, capacity for document delivery, etc.

5. That there should be maximum involvement of the private sector—nonprofit and profit-making—in the information network and in the general effort to improve library services. Tax credits should be provided for industries with extensive library and research facilities which make such facilities and collections available to the public. Sharing arrangements would have to cover five or ten year periods in order to qualify for the tax credit. Government incentive funding should be provided to stimulate cooperative ventures between libraries and private industries.

If the final legislation is saturated with these five concepts, a new framework—new parameters for the response of libraries to social change—will be established. The civil rights crisis did not end; it merely lost its high visibility as it moved from the streets into the courts. Litigation concerning discrimination in employment is now a primary civil rights activity. Litigation begins with information and research and therefore a network which provides access to the files of the National Civil Rights Commission through the local library is very much an instrument for social change. This example is applicable also to the environmental dangers crisis, the economic crisis and the energy crisis. Information for decision-making is needed and when libraries provide such information they become enzymes for social change: they speed up the process but are not themselves consumed.

SUMMARY AND CONCLUSIONS

In conclusion let me quote two giants. Winston Churchill stated that courage is the most important of all virtues because courage is necessary to preserve all of the other virtues. The contention of this presentation is that political action is a most important professional activity because the fruits of such efforts make so many other productive endeavors possible. In the centennial issue of *Library Journal*, the second giant, ALA President Clara Jones, indicated a similar belief when she called for a more political and organized attempt for libraries to meet the challenges that now face them.

In the White House Conference we are provided with the opportunity to launch this more political and organized attempt on a monumental scale. The White House Conference—both the vital process of preparation for it and the actual conference—must not become a monstrously splintered and fragmented circus. The need is for the conference to focus on the critical questions like a laser beam.

The hostility of public indifference—the poison of neglect—this is the negative violence destroying our libraries. The White House Conference provides us with a national arena where we may seize the initiative to eradicate this dangerous indifference and neglect. Sound proposals and imaginative strategies for implementing them will provide the inspiration and the impetus for libraries to break with the negative responses of the past and go forward as positive forces for social change. The choice for the profession is to meet the challenge or fade away. I do not think that we will fade away.

The Impact of Social Change on Libraries: A Literature Review

by Leigh Estabrook and
Thomas Blumenthal

In the preparation of this paper for the participants at the June, 1977 Conference of the American Library Association, to introduce them to the literature on the impact of social change on the library, the criteria for including materials were: that they relate directly to the given topic; and that they are not included in any other topic on which literature review papers were written. With this in mind, materials which consider changing management forms, library cooperation, intellectual freedom, information and referral centers, and a number of other areas which have felt the impact of social change, have not been included; nor has any general material on the nature of social change.

The books and articles which will be discussed below have been grouped into three categories: general works on the subject; works that consider the impact of social change on the library profession; and works that study the impact of social change on library and information services.

Of the general works on the impact of social change on the library, two have been written which provided an historical perspective. Jesse Shera, in "Plus Ça Change,"[26] looks back over several decades and analyzes the library's response to a number of critical events in American society. Shera concludes that social turmoil has frequently been met by the library profession with a greater concern for the profession itself than for the main currents of social life. Both the American Library Association as an organization and the members within it have seemed to respond time and again in a conservative manner.

Arthur Curley in his article from *Advances in Librarianship*[9] also views the library's response to social change in historical terms, but he concentrates on the past fifteen years. Arriving at conclusions similar to Shera's, Curley asserts that the library has responded belatedly to social change, and only after massive public outcries or federal funding have determined the directions in which librarianship should move. Thus only *after* the federal government funded outreach programs in the 1960s did the library begin to initiate and develop such programs. What Curley finds is an essentially confused response by libraries, resulting from conflicting definitions of what constitutes social responsibility and social change.

An excellent example of the confusion which Curley identifies can be found in some of the other general works on the impact of social change on libraries. Perhaps the foremost example was the "Berninghausen Debate." In the Fall of 1972, David Berninghausen published an article in *Library Journal* entitled "Social Responsibility vs. the Library Bill of Rights."[3] Berninghausen maintains that dealing with social issues (e.g., pollution, gay rights) is *not* a priority of the library and that the attempts by the ALA to respond to recent social problems have weakened the association. Berninghausen maintains that under a code of constant social responsibility, libraries would have to throw out all material they decide is not fully "responsible." He sees social responsibility as the antithesis of free access to information.

The response to Berninghausen was centered on the way in which he had defined social responsibility. A collection of opposing opinions was published under the title, "The Berninghausen Debate."[4] Included in it was Patricia Glass Schuman's essay which argued that social responsibility is not censorship but an attempt to bring to the public's attention less popular ideas. Clara Stanton Jones, too, argued that the Library Bill of Rights and the concept of social responsibility are not contradictory, and she asks the librarians to recognize the weight of their profession and to use the democratic forum provided by "social responsibility."

A related debate had occurred a few years earlier. In a symposium printed in the *Wilson Library Bulletin* and edited by Dorothy Bendix,[2] a group of librarians including Lucy Gorbey, Robert Wedgeworth, and Miriam Crawford attacked the question, "When is a Social Issue a Library Issue?" A reading of that symposium clearly demonstrates the lack within the profession of a common understanding of how to answer the question. Gorbey argues that the objectives of the library are information, education, and recreation and that the library has no business becoming a social welfare agency. Wedgeworth counters that libraries are shaped by political forces and cannot be impartial.

Consideration of this question occurs also in a number of other recent works, including Pings' "The Library as a Social Agency, Response to Social Change,"[21] and Wasserman's *The New Librarianship: A Challenge for Change.*[29]

Pings asserts that libraries serve as social agencies, and like all social agencies they become mired in internal rather than external concerns. As a result of their dependence on community support for funding, they often conform to community or institutional pressure, rather than defining their own objectives. Pings states that little research has been done on the entire question of change and the methods of bringing it about. Significant response to social change comes institutionally, yet little research has been done on the meaning and effect of institutional change. Emphasizing the enormous potential librarians have for decision making, Pings says that they have not realized the importance of assessing the availability of information and defining objectives.

A number of the points made by Pings are echoed by Wasserman. Wasserman believes that libraries are failing because they are tied to the past. Their programs and policies have emphasized institutional values rather than public service ones. Like Pings, Wasserman recognizes that change is often related to organizational structure; but he expands his analysis to include consideration of sociological, political, psychological, economic, and educational factors which also affect library response to social change. He stresses the need for a new direction in library leadership which will utilize more participatory management and will alter present values from acquiring and processing of materials to include human needs.

Two other works, *Library Issues: The Sixties*[20] and *Social Responsibility and Libraries*,[24] provide a wider framework for understanding the various positions taken on the impact of social change on libraries. In the words of the introduction to *Library Issues*, they provide the "source material of history."

Patricia Glass Schuman's compilation entitled *Social Responsibility and Libraries*[24] draws on *Library Journal/School Library Journal* material. The work includes articles that appeared between 1968 and 1976 and relate to the "personal, professional, and institutional programs which attempt to deal with the implementation of social responsibility." To the extent that "social responsibility" is only one dimension of the impact of social change on the library, *Social Responsibility and Libraries* provides insight into a variety of views on the subject.

Finally, within the category of general works on the impact of social change on libraries, two theoretical works have been published which should be mentioned. G. M. Smith's "Sociology and Librarianship"[28] argues that issues within the library profession are infrequently analyzed from a sociological perspective. Too often the profession reacts to change as a given factor rather than investigating the social environment that allows and causes change. Thus the academic library will try to assess students' motivations and activities, but few attempts are made to determine the underlying bases for their behavior. It is crucial, Smith argues, for professional librarians to see, that just as they can aid other disciplines, so other disciplines (e.g., sociology) can be of enormous help in coming to terms with the issues of social change that continually surround the library and librarians.

The second of the important theoretical works was also written by a British scholar. Ronald Benge in *Communication and Identity*[1] offers a thoughtful analysis of the issues involved in response to social change and raises questions that the members of any institution must respond to before assessing their own response to change. Benge asserts that there is a resistance on the part of the library establishment to the disorder that is implicit in change because of an institutional bias toward rationalism and the preservation of the *status quo.* Social change demands that we break free from the assumptions given a local habitation and a name in existing institutions. Benge recognizes the difficulty in such a break—our identities are wrapped up in our institutional roles—but cautions that maintaining these same institutional roles affords us an easy way to avoid facing the complexities of change.

The works discussed above provide a general foundation for looking at the impact of social change on libraries. They consider the problem from a variety of points of view and are not limited to certain groups of librarians or to specific types of libraries. The books and articles which will now be considered treat more specific aspects of the problem.

The impact of social change on the profession has been significant in recent years. Within the parameters of this paper, two specific areas will be considered: the role of the Black librarian, and the role of women in librarianship. For an understanding of the changing role of the Black librarian, two books edited by E. J. Josey provide the best background. *The Black Librarian in America*[15] includes a number of short—frequently autobiographical—essays that focus on a search for identity for the Black librarian in library education, public, academic, and special libraries, and government agencies. Made clear in the collection is the way in which the politics of existing institutions frequently deny to Black librarians the possibility of having a great impact on their field.

Josey's second collection, *What Black Librarians are Saying,*[16] is a more detailed, analytical approach to the way in which library issues affect the Black librarian. Many of the articles are equally relevant for Black and White librarians—for example, Walter Fraser's article which raises the problem of the conflict between institutional and professional goals. Other points include the persistence of White control of libraries in Black communities, the failure of library schools to recruit or train a significant number of Black students, and the need for all librarians to be more aggressive in their approach to conflict.

No comparable compilation on the subject of women in librarianship has as of now been published, although Kathleen Weibel and Kathleen M. Heim are presently preparing one for The Oryx Press. The three articles discussed below do, however, provide a good historical overview of the topic and a review of available statistical data.

Schiller's[23] article from *Advances in Librarianship* is perhaps the most definitive of the several she has published. In it she provides a detailed analysis of salaries, professional experience, academic degrees, and administrative positions of female librarians, and she compares these data with those from other professional groups. She considers the specific problems women face in regard to unionization, education, and mobility; and she looks toward potential change in light of ALA positions on the status of women and affirmative action. Schiller's study provides a valuable look at the myriad factors that affect the status of women. She refuses to deal with the problem in isolation and recognizes the complexity of the issue and the great amount of work yet to be done.

In "Toward a Feminist Profession," Kathleen Weibel[30] looks at the relationship between the women's movement and the library profession, noting that organized women's activities have come later to librarianship than to other professions. This has been true despite the fact that the library profession is expected to remain female-intensive for at least the next quarter century. Weibel observes that the stereotype of female characteristics is often seen as very similar to that of the librarian's characteristics, especially when librarianship is regarded as emphasizing humanitarian service rooted in emotions and a task rather than an intellectual orientation. She strongly believes that, by attacking these stereotypes, the women's movement can contribute to better developed and better organized libraries. In opposition to both stereotypes, librarians should be concerned with equality of relationships, participatory rather than mechanistic management, development of the individual and the collective, and responsibility rather than dependency. For these goals to be reached, a tremendous amount of work will be required from women within the profession, and the profession as a whole will have to change.

Complementary to Weibel's article is that of Antje Lemke entitled "Access, Barriers, Change: the ABC's of Women in Libraries."[17] Lemke relates the status of women in the library profession to the status of women in society at large and presents an historical analysis to illustrate the parallels. Between 1870 and World War I, many women were involved in library administration—a mirror of a strong feminist movement in this country. After World War I, as Freud's views on women became dominant, and perhaps partially as a result of those views, the status of women in society saw little growth. The same was true in librarianship. Lemke notes that at the present time women's salaries and status within the profession are low. She directs the reader's attention to actions necessary to remedy existing inequalities: affirmative action legal proceedings, increased recruitment of women and minorities into library schools, continuing education for women, and a stronger stand on these issues by the ALA.

When one turns to the literature of the impact of social change on the library, one finds a much larger range of materials. Generally, these can be grouped by type of library, but there are exceptions: no good general work on the impact of social change on special libraries seems to have been published; and a large body of material exists on the urban library as a special case.

On the subject of the impact of social change on academic libraries, two articles should be considered. The first is Richard Lyman's "New Trends in Higher Education: The Impact on the University Library,"[18] in which Lyman argues that change within the university and the urban community at large have far-reaching implications for the university library. Within academia, required courses are being deemphasized, interdisciplinary ones are being stressed. This has led to a demand by users for the library to commit financial resources to purchase more international indexes, abstracts, and bibliographic tools. At the same time, libraries are moving toward increased cooperation with other libraries. From the outside community, university libraries are facing pressure from individuals who are involved in the various "continuing" and "life long" education movements. As those outside the traditional academic community place pressure on the university library, users will become more diverse in age, ethnicity, and social and economic background. University libraries, Lyman argues, must be willing to shift emphasis according to expressed demands, to consider becoming more of a "community library," and to be willing to accept the fact that as they choose to expand in one area, they will have to contract in others.

Jessie Carney Smith[27] provides a specific example of one of Lyman's points as she examines the "Impact of Black Studies Programs on the Academic Library." In her article Smith demonstrates the consequences of libraries responding to the pressures of social change. Black Studies programs were developed in response to the 1960s quest by minority groups for self definition. Three distinct types of programs emerged: (1) the separatist, (2) the interdisciplinary, and (3) the integrated. Smith does not take a stand for any one particular approach, but she does contend that academic libraries have not responded well to any of these. Afro-American collections have been hastily developed, often by people with little expertise who are acting under pressure. In the future, Smith argues that libraries must plan for change, rather than simply reacting to it.

Some of the same pressures faced by academic libraries have also been confronted in schools, but school libraries have, in addition, problems unique to their institutional framework.

Lillian Shapiro's book, *Serving Youth*,[25] focuses specifically on the media center in high schools. She notes that these libraries could be as valuable to their students as a special library is to its clients, but that they lack the intellectual stature of academic and public libraries and the identifiable value of special libraries. As schools are affected by changing family structure, television, teachers' roles, and religion, the process of communication in the school and in the media center has been altered. School libraries are being asked to change, but to do so will require a reexamination of library education and current library leadership.

More limited in scope is Cheatham's "Reflections in Library Developments and Setbacks in 1976."[7] This article provides a valuable chronicle of the social and political events of 1976 which affected school libraries—high unemployment, low tax revenues, and cuts in city budgets which necessitated maintenance rather than expansion of services. Cheatham observes that within school media centers many librarians' positions were terminated, there were frequent conflicts with school boards, and parents often fought to become censors of the reading material provided to their children. On this last point, Cheatham notes as pivotal events the Island Trees case concerning intellectual freedom, publishers' stands on the "right to read" and "need to know," and the ALA debates on racism and sexism.

Cheatham's point on school libraries is one that is repeatedly made in the literature on the impact of social change on public libraries. The individual who has published most extensively on the historical dimensions of this problem is Michael Harris.[13] The most recent of his articles is "Public Libraries and the Decline of the Democratic Dogma." In it he continues his argument that theories of the early history of public libraries which claim the library was an egalitarian, libertarian institution fail to recognize the motivation of early library founders to control and direct the behavior of the people the library was to serve. Harris attributes current hostility toward the public library by its former supporters to a loss of faith in democratic dogma—to disillusionment with education as a means of getting ahead. Harris believes that librarians must look to library history in order to adapt to future social changes.

One of the major responses to Harris' theory has come from Phyllis Dain.[10] In her "Ambivalence and Paradox: The Social Bonds of the Public Library," she agrees with one of Harris' assertions—that public library boards are not representative of the total community or its library users—but she does not believe this situation necessarily results in an ill-served community. She, too, draws on historical evidence and believes that the response of the public library to social change is related to the prevailing ideology of the times as well as to economic and political concerns; but she is much less willing to see the public library as a failure.

Boyd Rayward[22] uses library history in a way dramatically different from that of either Harris or Dain. Rayward argues that one frequently finds two positions toward public library response to social change: either it is seen as valid and imperative or it is viewed as an abdication of tradition and principles. Such a rigid dichotomy is not justified, argues Rayward, who believes that current responses to social change are not discontinuous with the past. New programs such as Learner's Advisor and Information and Referral are in fact alterations of older programs such as Reader's Advisor and traditional reference service, respectively. Recognition of this continuity would, he believes, result in greater support for new programs from members of the library profession and alter the present situation in which support for most new programs seems to come from outside the profession.

One specific aspect of public library response to social change is discussed in Larry Bone's article, "The Public Library Goals and Objectives Movement: Death Gasp or Renaissance."[6] Bone sees the "goals and objectives movement" as one response to social change in the 1960s, one which has been dealt with more easily in small libraries than large. Larger libraries are handicapped in setting goals by problems in getting the input of the entire staff, without which resistance to implementation is likely to occur. Large urban public libraries must contend with political factors which often militate against effective planning. Library planning is often based on generalities rather than specific priorities because of fear that less vital but still important programs might be eliminated. Bone recognizes the difficulty in formulating well-articulated goals and objectives, but he contends that, under the pressures of rapid change, libraries must take the initiative, rather than waiting for pressure from others.

During the 1960s and '70s, urban areas were particularly affected by the social changes of the time. It is not surprising that a significant portion of the literature on the impact of social change on the libraries has been devoted to the specific case of urban libraries.

A straightforward and thorough case study of one urban library was directed by Lowell Martin and reported in his book, *Library Response to Urban Change: A Study of the Chicago Public Library*.[19] Martin claims that the areas which were being emphasized at Chicago Public—services to children and students and circulation of "middle range" publications for adults—will decline in the future. As an alternative, it will be necessary to develop specialized target programs, advanced resources for nonuniversity specialists, and information services and self-development programs for the urban underprivileged. The report urges that professional librarians should avoid trying to do all things: many jobs that they now perform could best be handled by specialists.

A more general analysis of the issues raised in Martin's study can be found in John Frantz's[11] article on the urban library, Clara Stanton Jones' "The Urban Public Library: Proving Utility,"[14] and the entire October 1971 *Library Trends* issue. Frantz specifies a number of dimensions of social change in urban areas which should be responded to by urban libraries. He urges libraries to be in the forefront of dealing with the high illiteracy rate, consumer and drug problems; he also proposes that community policy boards should decide on library materials, hours and programs.

Jones stresses that libraries during periods of change must build on existing values and recognize new ideas. Too often library programs designed to meet changing social conditions continue, not because of demonstrated value, but because of momentum and committed librarians. Jones makes a strong statement in favor of information and referral services which she believes can provide a base from which to prove library utility and thereby increase funding. Jones calls for a more political and organized attempt for libraries to meet the challenges that now face them.

The issue of *Library Trends* on "Current Trends in Urban Main Libraries"[5] also looks at urban social change and the library's response to it, but in a more detailed fashion. One of the major points dealt with in several of the essays is the pressure on urban libraries to maintain both the major reference collection for the city and neighborhood branch service for inner-city residents. Lowell Martin, in his article, develops more fully his idea that the urban main library should stop trying to do everything—that instead it should develop specialized services to specific user groups.

Two other monographs on this subject provide more integrated analyses. Judith Guthman[12] provides a brief general survey of the problems and potential of metropolitan libraries. She argues that libraries have not done enough for the poor, and she calls for increased funding for this purpose. Local government frequently supports the *status quo* and the library, as part of that government, is often forced to work toward similar ends. Guthman explores the socio-economic realities of the city in contrast to the suburb, profiles the city users, and outlines specific outreach programs. She also surveys a variety of interrelated issues that concern not just metropolitan libraries but all libraries. These issues include the area-wide library concept, cooperative arrangements, and the need for more staff and innovative programs.

A more expanded consideration of the metropolitan library is provided by a book by that name, edited by Conant and Molz[8] and newly revised in 1976. Included are essays on the history of the metropolitan library, characteristics of urban society, the financing of metropolitan libraries, the urban disadvantaged, and metropolitan politics and government. Conant evaluates the potential effect of the educational evolution on libraries. Dan Lacy looks at the need for libraries and urban schools to provide information to the less literate. The collection provides, in greater detail than any of the other works discussed in this section, a thorough foundation for analyzing metropolitan libraries and the environment within which they function. In reading them it becomes clear that, while the problem of social change was most frequently debated in the late 1960s and early '70s, it remains unresolved.

REFERENCES

1. Benge, Ronald. *Communication and Identity*. Linnet Books, 1972.
2. Bendix, Dorothy, ed. "When is a Social Issue a Library Issue," *Wilson Library Bulletin* 45:43-61 (1970).

3. Berninghausen, David. "Social Responsibility vs. the Library Bill of Rights," *Library Journal* 97:3675-81 (November 15, 1972).
4. The Berninghausen Debate, *Library Journal* (January 1, 1973).
5. Bone, Larry Earl, ed. "Current Trends in Urban Main Libraries," *Library Trends* 20:595-774 (April 1972).
6. _____. "The Public Library Goals and Objectives Movement: Death Gasp or Renaissance?" *Library Journal* 100:1283-86 (July 1975).
7. Cheatham, Bertha M. "Reflections on Library Developments and Setbacks in 1976," *School Library Journal* 23:21-25 (December 1976).
8. Conant, Ralph W. and Molz, Kathleen, eds. *The Metropolitan Library*. Cambridge, MA: MIT Press, 1976.
9. Curley, Arthur. "Social Responsibility and the Libraries," *Advances in Librarianship* 4:77-101 (1974).
10. Dain, Phyllis, "Ambivalence and Paradox: The Social Bonds of the Public Library," *Library Journal* 100:261-66 (February 1, 1975).
11. Frantz, John C. "The Changing Environment and Changing Institution: The Urban Library," *Library Trends* 20: 367-375 (October 1971).
12. Guthman, Judith Dommu. *Metropolitan Libraries: The Challenge and the Promise*. American Library Association, 1969.
13. Harris, Michael H. "Public Libraries and the Decline of the Democratic Dogma," *Library Journal* 101:2225-30 (November 1, 1976).
14. Jones, Clara Stanton. "The Urban Public Library: Proving Utility," *Library Journal* 101:81-6 (January 1, 1976).
15. Josey, E. J., ed. *The Black Librarian in America*. Metuchen, NJ: Scarecrow Press, 1970.
16. _____. *What Black Librarians are Saying*. Metuchen, NJ: Scarecrow Press, 1972.
17. Lemke, Antje B. "Access, Barriers, Change: the ABC's of Women in Libraries," *School Library Journal* 22:17-19 (January 1976).
18. Lyman, Richard W. "New Trends in Higher Education: The Impact on the University Library," *College and Research Libraries* 33:298-304 (July 1972).
19. Martin, Lowell A. *Library Response to Urban Change: A Study of the Chicago Public Library*. Chicago: American Library Association, 1969.
20. Moon, Eric and Nyren, Karl, eds. *Library Issues: the Sixties*. New York: Bowker, 1970.

21. Pings, Vern M. "The Library as a Social Agency, Response to Social Change," *College and Research Libraries* 31:174-84 (May 1970).
22. Rayward, W. Boyd. "Imperative of Change Effect Versus the Band Wagon Effect: Two Recent Developments in Public Librarianship," *Catholic Library World* 47:291-293 (Fall 1976).
23. Schiller, Anita. "Women in Librarianship," *Advances in Librarianship* 4:103-141 (1974).
24. Schuman, Patricia Glass, ed. *Social Responsibilities and Libraries.* New York: Bowker, 1976.
25. Shapiro, Lillian L. *Serving Youth: Communication and Commitment in the High School.* New York: Bowker, 1975.
26. Shera, Jesse H. "Plus Ca Change." *Library Journal* 95(6):979-986 (March 15, 1970).
27. Smith, Jessie Carney. "Impact of Black Studies Programs on the Academic Library," *College and Research Libraries* 33:87-96 (March 1972).
28. Smith, G. M. "Sociology and Librarianship," *ASLIB Proceedings* 25:234-242 (July 1973).
29. Wasserman, Paul. *The New Librarianship: A Challenge for Change.* New York: Bowker, 1972.
30. Weibel, Kathleen. "Towards a Feminist Profession," *Library Journal* 101:263-67 (January 1, 1976).

The Impact of Economic Change on Libraries

by Thomas R. Buckman

> Information is a name for the content of what is exchanged with the outer world as we adjust to it, and make our adjustments felt upon it. The process of receiving and of using information is the process of our adjusting to the contingencies of the outer environment. The needs and the complexity of modern life make greater demands on this process of information than ever before, and our press, our museums, our scientific laboratories, our universities, our libraries and textbooks, are obliged to meet the needs of this process or fail in their purpose. To live effectively is to live with adequate information.
>
> Norbert Wiener[14]

Norbert Wiener's definition of information and statement of its value implies some of the major questions of economic importance facing libraries: Is information a public good? How are information systems to be funded? What are the economic implications of information technology? What happens in the economy when the whole society becomes an information environment?

Pure Public Goods

Receiving and using information is a process necessary to life which is going on all the time through the senses unaided by technology and its extensions.

This process, in the economic sense, is a pure public good; its cost is completely unaffected by the number of people who have access to it.

It is a given fact of human functioning. It is, as economists say, "nonexcludable." It cannot be denied to anyone.

Because no price can be charged for it, there is no way its supply can be controlled, permitting it to become an article of commerce.

Observation and learning through seeing, hearing, and feeling, that is to say, by immediate and direct experience, is everyone's birthright. By exchanging verbal and nonverbal cues with that interesting person sitting across the table from you, you can engage in the information process at zero marginal cost.

Another form of pure public good is that class of desirable things which society determines it will provide to everyone, and by so doing cannot exclude from anyone, such as the benefits of national defense or the useful products of research.[3] The control of disease is an example. Everyone benefits by it automatically, even those who do not share in the cost by, for example, paying taxes. Because no one can be kept from having a public good through unwillingness to pay its price, there is no way its supply can be financed by private enterprise. Obviously no entrepreneur goes into the business of supplying national defense because there is no possibility of a return on investment. Therefore, government finances pure public goods.

Factors of Production in Recorded Information

Even though most of the information which we receive and use in order to adjust to the contingencies of the outer environment is informal, immediate, and direct, we in this profession usually limit the term to include only recorded information. Is such information a pure public good? The answer seems to be no. When we begin to record, organize, and disseminate information we introduce such factors as labor, materials, and technologies. The technologies can be as simple as parchment, pen and ink and become more complex as we move along a scale from printing presses, publishing houses, bookstores, libraries using conventional means, toward electronic applications.

The factors of production introduce costs which are affected by the number of persons served, and the information products do become excludable because they may be denied consumers unwilling to pay their price, as would be the case with a pair of shoes or a package of cereal. Market conditions intervene, and the information product takes on at least some of the character of a normal private good.

Subsidizing the Costs

At this point society may decide that all recorded information or certain types of recorded information should indeed be freely available as a public good for general educational and cultural purposes or to serve a democratic political philosophy. Public subsidies are then required.

Mixed Goods

But those who make decisions about the supply of the subsidy may begin to reason that the provision of all recorded information under a public subsidy may not be necessary. It is too costly, granted that there should be enough freely provided information to educate the young and perhaps all individuals throughout their lives; to provide cultural enrichment and vision; to enlighten the electorate, and for the general welfare. Still, the line must be drawn somewhere. Money and resources are always in short supply given the whole range of human and social needs.

The decision makers may conclude, with sufficient reason, that recorded information is not uniformly a public good; as in the case of education, performing arts, and museums, libraries and other information services which are the natural extensions of recorded information and are, in the economist's term, "mixed goods," having the qualities of both public and private goods. It is reasonable to believe, isn't it, that when someone goes to the library for information, his or her own welfare (including future earning ability) is thereby increased? Therefore, the argument goes, the individual should bear part of the cost according to some measure of use. Surely the information obtained yields benefits specifically to the individual which are distinguishable from the benefits which enrich the society as a whole.

If you accept this distinction, then you have the basis for charging for some services. If you reject the distinction, then you argue that all recorded information should be freely available under public subsidy.

Funding: Factors Affecting Decision-Making

It is easier to make the case for the distinction between certain uses of information and to charge than it is to reject it and argue for the undifferentiated supply of all recorded information under full public subsidy. Given the competition for public funds, it is likely that the question will be raised more often by public authorities who may take the view that free and universal access to all recorded information is unrealistic and that social goals can be achieved without it. Those who fund information systems—including libraries—will also give their attention to the relative costs and capacities of the technologies, and will increasingly opt for those which are cost beneficial, again assuming that social needs will not be shortchanged.

The economics of the new technologies will not only affect libraries directly, but also indirectly, because the economic trends and technological applications have become widespread throughout the economy and will make obvious the relative rates of development and effectiveness of library and nonlibrary information systems. We can observe an information-based economy growing up around libraries and extending far beyond them. The rates of development in other information sectors are proceeding very rapidly and will have a challenging impact on us.

Consider the wide variety of information service markets whose end product is knowledge.

> An information market enables the consumer to know something that was not known beforehand; to exchange a symbolic experience; to learn or relearn something; to change perception or cognition; to reduce uncertainty; to expand one's range of options; to exercise rational choice; to evaluate decisions; to control a process; and to communicate an idea, a fact or an opinion. An information market may sell topical knowledge with a very short useful life; it may exchange long lasting knowledge. It may involve a completely specialized or unique con-

figuration of knowledge, useful to only one person in one situation, or it may be public knowledge available to all simultaneously and generally useful in many contexts. It could be extremely costly to produce, or it may involve only very simple processing and transmission approaching zero marginal cost. Information could be a lengthy process spanning a whole lifetime (such as invention), or it could be a burst of data occurring in a millionth of a second.[9]

Library services cannot encompass all of the knowledge uses which the society demands. Or can they?

We occupy a relatively small place in the economy. We are one of the smaller information markets accounting at best for two- to three-tenths of one percent of the GNP, and not quite one percent of that portion of GNP attributable to the information sector broadly defined. Although our role is perhaps a unique one, we cannot expect that its traditional boundaries will be preserved. Under the economic pressures of technological change, the provision of information through other channels, many of them fee-based, may preempt some of our functions. The information economy will require us to reexamine what we are doing year by year and to concentrate our resources on the things which we can do better than anyone else.

The mixed good characteristic of library services, and the economics of advancing technology will force a continuing study of how libraries are to be funded and of what portion of information services is to be paid for by end users.

Looking Ahead: Some Generalizations

Subject to the hazards of prediction, and the better knowledge which many of you have, I will, in the remaining part of this paper, try to look ahead twenty to twenty-five years and generalize on the economics of the competing information technologies as they relate to libraries, the economic and social advantages of an information society and, finally, describe the information-based economy emerging around us and some of the policy issues which it poses.

Little attention will be given to short-term economic problems of libraries; change is proceeding so rapidly that most attention should be given to longer term objectives of libraries and means of affecting national policy.

In the short term we seem to face a holding situation, that is, in the pessimistic view, the management of decline in an era of retrenchment. Most libraries are experiencing a financial crisis characterized by rising costs, a labor-intensive manual technology, complexity of organization, increasing social need, and the dilemma of greater deficits if service is extended to more people. However, this may be recast optimistically as a situation specially favorable to creative responses.

Principal Costs

Libraries have a disadvantageous postion in the economy now because their principal operating costs are for staffing and materials.

Both are rising steadily in price in an inflationary market with no end in sight. The various theories which attempt to explain the causes of inflation, whichever of them you choose to believe, all seem to indicate that inflation will be a continuing fact of life. Libraries must find ways of reducing these rising costs to increase productivity expressed as the ratio of output to the amount of input required to produce it.

Short-Term Application of Technology

Over the short run, the application of technology for the purpose of reducing unit costs appears to be prohibitive. We can't reduce staff and purchases sufficiently to be able to afford the major technologies. There have been significant advances in the development of library networks, but as yet they have not reached their full potential. Many libraries are without any network connection. At the same time, outmoded technologies in the nonlibrary information sector place great financial burdens on libraries, for example, in journal publishing.

Complexity of Information Needs

The social, scientific, and humanistic information requirements which libraries exist to serve are increasingly complex at every level of library service and, therefore, more costly. Twenty or thirty years ago, one individual might be able to encompass the information needed, but today the same problems may require specialists, and interdisciplinary work drawing on sources not only in our own country but around the world. This is reflected in the proliferation of new publications. There is a need for more information resources to tackle the same needs and problems at the same time as the tools for dealing with them become more sophisticated.

Reaching More Users Means Greater Costs

Libraries are beginning to benefit by economies of scale—for example, in processing—but inevitably when there are more users there must be higher materials budgets and more service staff and, therefore, costs expand in proportion to the number of people served. Success in meeting information needs may also, ironically, result in larger deficits given the present structure of libraries.

Funding Sources for Libraries Face Economic Problems

The sources of funding for most libraries are facing economic problems of their own. Not only New York, but many other American cities are losing the capacity to earn enough money to support their present populations, and to provide necessary services. Manufacturing industries are moving out, and the population is declining in the central cities. There have been cutbacks in essential areas, such as fire and police protection, and health services and, of course, these have also affected public and school libraries. University systems are in a no-growth period. Two essentials are no longer in ready supply: money and students. How to structure the systems for the coming decade is vigorously debated. College and university libraries in both public and private institutions are feeling the pinch. Many special libraries faced cutbacks or phasing out in recent years because of uncertain business futures and a wavering stock market. Private giving by individuals, foundations, and corporations in terms of purchasing power is not keeping pace with the growth of the economy, and has fallen off absolutely when discounted for inflation.

Economic Implications of Technological Development

Against this background of economic difficulties of libraries, consider the wider setting of the new information society. Familiar information technologies, already within the last twenty years, "have become an indispensable part of the web that holds society together," but only in the past four or five years have we begun to realize that they are more than just another consumption or luxury item, and may be, in the future, the chief basis for productivity gains in the economy as a whole.

The Cost of Technology Over the Long Run

In the long run, libraries may be able to take better advantage of this more general trend in the economy. While the cost per unit of library services has been rising steadily relative to the average cost of commodities, the cost of computer and telecommunication equipment has been steadily falling at the same time that their capabilities have been increasing.

Economic Necessity

In 1973, Baumol stated

> With recent rates of change in their costs continuing, only a decade would be required to eliminate a ten-fold operational cost differential between service activity and a purely electronic substitute (assuming a purely electronic substitute exists or can be developed). By the time two decades had passed, the cost of the labor intensive conventional process would have risen to twenty times that of its electronic substitute.[2]

Aronofsky and Korfhage predict in their March 1977 article in the *Journal of Library Automation* that

> . . . there seems to be no doubt that the increasing volume of information resources and the decreasing cost of . . . equipment and services will drive a library network system to the point of being cost effective well within the next five years.[1]

Opportunity and Stress

In speaking of computer networks providing services for colleges, universities, and high schools, the same authors note that ". . . some of the networks have been highly successful and others have failed. Failure has been primarily due to organizational difficulties rather than to technical problems."[1] This comment points to a significant obstacle. There is clearly an opportunity to restructure library operations spurred by economic crisis and technological change, but there will be tensions within libraries as they are forced to adapt to or defend themselves against the technologies.

The condition is fairly widespread. The Conference Board report states "Fear of information technology is an aggravating element in the current rejection by dissenting groups of large and complex organizations, whether business, governmental, or educational . . . [But] if large numbers of Americans, including some who are spokesmen and leaders, continue to fear and distrust the technologies that the society will not abandon, then the basic morale, the self-confidence and cohesion of United States society would be gravely impaired."[13] Some librarians facing technology seem to be much like the honors English major who, upon being informed at registration that she would need to take a basic math course to graduate, burst into tears because "her entire self-concept had been attacked."[11]

In any discussion of the information society as narrowly focused as this one, the fear might well arise that "the current enlightenment of the epoch" will overlook the need to maintain the past in "a dignified independent existence of its own." As Gordon Ray has said

> The central work of keeping the past available in current form is carried on for the most part in colleges and universities, in independent research libraries and museums, and in centers for advanced study . . . The results of this continuous process of investigation, analysis, and synthesis are made available through books and journals published by university presses and trade houses of scholarly orientation. The massive structure of organized learning thus achieved has become so familiar a part of the contemporary scene that its invulnerability is taken for granted. Publishers of popular books and magazines assume that it will continue to provide them with data in profusion. The entertainment and advertising industries see it as an unfailing source for the retrospective materials that they need. Unfortunately this vast apparatus of learning is by no means an unalterable fact of nature.[10]

One would certainly agree that the record of the past must be preserved and must be accessible, but whether the "massive structure" and "vast apparatus" can be justified is another question. The way may be difficult, but acceptable technological applications must surely be found to enhance humanistic values. The economic strains are perhaps more severe in these areas than in any others.

Analysis of Library Services to Meet Social Needs

Tears will not help. A better response would be the analysis of the alternatives the technology offers that will make possible the restructuring of libraries and other information activities so that they may better serve social aims. This is certainly in the mainstream of concerns which so many librarians have expressed so emphatically in recent years. The opportunities transcend the uses of information and could help us to create a more livable society free of much of the menacing clutter that surrounds us now.

Energy, Environment, and Growth Limits

Two economic policy issues of great social import are energy and the environment. Recent Carter Administration proposals vividly illustrate the point. Restrictions limiting physical growth, i.e., of manufactured products, are near at hand. Edwin B. Parker states the problem:

> Economic planners can no longer assume an unlimited potential supply of energy and materials. Material shortages and increased energy costs, as well as increased public concern for the negative ecological effects of continued growth and energy consumption and unrecycled materials, have forced economic planners to face the possibility of real limits to physical growth. Future economic growth must be planned with more severe constraints on increases in energy consumption and consumption of nonrenewable resources. It will depend on 'working smarter' rather than 'working harder.' We appear to be at the beginning of a long social transition to a state of zero population growth and a more stable ecology. (Some would say that the human species will not survive unless some success is achieved in approaching such goals.) The long-term focus of policies for economic growth (or further improvements in the quality of life, however measured) must be on how to achieve more output per unit of input of materials and energy rather than how to increase the supply of inputs.[8]

This is precisely what an information society could do.

Fred Hirsch in his book *Social Limits to Growth*[4] distinguishes between the kind of products whose enjoyments are wholly divorced from the number of persons who are consuming them, and what he calls "positional goods" whose enjoyments for the individual depend on not too many other people having them. Information is a good example of the first type. There is no reason why an infinitely large number of people cannot use and benefit by information without interfering with the use and benefit that others derive from it.

A house with a view and automobiles are examples of "positional" goods. The satisfactions derived from having them are directly affected by how many others have them. They are goods whose enjoyments depend on the fact that they are owned by a minority. Their advantages disappear when they are owned by a majority. The analogy, as Hirsch says, is to standing on tiptoe in a crowd. The advantage works for a few but is self-defeating for all. The acquisitive aim of accumulating "positional" goods cannot be made to conform to democratic principles. It weakens economic performance, and undermines the social fabric. Thus, there are also persuasive social and political reasons for limiting growth.

The Economic Promise of Information

The limits of growth imposed by finite supplies of energy, preservation of the environment, and social contradictions might cause us anxiety as we look at our economy were it not for the fact that there is the possibility of unlimited economic growth of information products and services not entailing any of these dilemmas. An economy based on the production of information can, assuming a well-designed national policy, alleviate energy shortages and environmental problems, and create a learning society in which libraries in their new forms would have a natural place consonant with the aspirations of the profession.

As memory units and logic circuits decrease in size and in cost with relatively higher capacity, more information can be manipulated with less use of energy and materials. Add to that a national electronic network and you begin to envision a society in which people derive their livelihoods, social effectiveness, and personal satisfactions from the use of information preferentially, rather than through as much consumption as previously of goods requiring high inputs of energy and materials. It would be a society in which people and physical objects are moved around less in space. Instead, information would be moved and would be the primary activity. This does not mean that our familiar world of physical objects, travel and consumption would disappear and that we would all become contemplatives, but that industrial production and use would not be the primary focus.

ECONOMIC TRENDS INDICATE A RAPID ADVANCE TOWARD AN INFORMATION SOCIETY

The idea of an information society had its origin with Fritz Machlup fifteen years ago, and many aspects of it have been dealt with by others since that time. The starting point in defining what we see as an emerging information society is an examination of by now familiar economic trends in this country and abroad.

Work Force, National Income, and Consumption

The chief indicators are[8]

(1) Distribution of the labor force,

(2) Trends in the components of the national income,

(3) Trends in personal consumption.

Nearly fifty percent of the work force in the United States today is employed in information activities, i.e., those primarily concerned with symbol-processing activities or with the production or maintenance of machines for symbol manipulation.

One-third to one-half of the gross national product is now attributable to the production, processing and use of information.

About one-third of all personal consumption is now allocated to information goods and services defined as: telephone, private education, books, magazines, radio, TV, motion pictures, theater, and personal business such as legal, financial and counseling services.

Porat has defined the information economy in extensive detail.[11] His typology of information industries in the primary information sector is organized under four main headings:

  I. *Markets for Information,* including knowledge production and inventive industries and information distribution and communications industries

 II. *Information in Markets,* including search and coordination industries, risk management industries

III. *Information Infrastructure,* including information processing and transmission services, information goods manufacturing industries

 IV. *Wholesale and Retail Trade in Information Goods.* "The unifying definition is that the goods and services that make up the primary sector must be fundamentally valued for their information producing, processing, or distributing characteristics."[9] Included are a wide variety of industries not usually thought of as information handling organizations, such as banking, accounting, advertising, insurance, but which nonetheless fit Porat's definition. Although they are heterogeneous industries, they sell to each other, support each other, and together behave as a "sector."

A secondary information sector includes the public and private bureaucracies of noninformation organizations with their own information producing, processing, or distributing capabilities. Together, the two sectors accounted for forty-six percent of GNP in 1967.

The information economy is not a monolith. It is, after all, our old familiar economy, or rather the largest part of it redefined by new technological possibilities, and presented to us as the dominant economic force in our country. There is great diversity within it, different starting situations, rates of growth, and different goals. The perception of its development depends on where you stand in the information work force. Thus, we have the simplistic, visionary, or limited views which gain wide circulation when observers in one branch of the work force make predictions for all information-based organizations often in a rigid, deterministic way. But the new technology will not go away and, because of its economics and flexible variety of applications, it will almost certainly restructure to greater or lesser degree every type of organization based on the production, dissemination, or use of information.

How Did It Happen?

There are apparently three reasons for the explosive growth of information activities during the past thirty years, according to Parker.[8]

(1) The underlying technology of computers, transistors, integrated circuits, and the like. The great reduction in the unit costs of information products and services as a result of these technological changes has led to a greater demand for information products and services, both as final products (consumption items) and as intermediate products useful in the production of other goods and services (e.g., computer services within other businesses). The lower unit costs for information processing have made possible new kinds of activities not previously possible or economically viable. Hence, the lowering of unit costs has led to increases in expenditure on information.

(2) A second reason may be that increased expenditure on information activities (even labor intensive ones such as education which have not had the benefit of cost-reducing technology) has led to economic productivity gains in the rest of the economy.

(3) A third reason may be increased use of information because of market inefficiencies. For example, expenditures on advertising may contribute little to the value of advertised products, because of counter-productive competition within industries. In this regard, Geoffrey Vickers suggests another possible benefit in an advanced information society.[12] Reliable information on all existing products of interest to consumers would be available from a central data bank for comparison. The system would cost no more than present expenditures for advertising which would no longer be necessary. Consumers would be better served and producers of better mousetraps would be rewarded more quickly. This would tend to bring about the classical condition of perfect competition in the market.

Popular Consciousness: Another Indicator

More evidence of the emergence of an information society is found in articles in media and professional publications. These are usually not put in a broad economic context. Rather, they suggest sweeping changes within familiar institutions. Many readers may be startled, but have little idea of how these converging examples fit into the larger picture. These examples also show the drastic restructuring that will take place in types of organizations much larger and more pervasive in the economy than libraries. If it will happen to them, how can it not happen to libraries?

Here is a sampling based on casual reading during the past few months:

Item: March 1977   "Electronic Money," Eastern Airlines magazine, *Review*

Before long, the article says, the average American will be able to complete most financial transactions, twenty-four hours a day, with nothing more than a little plastic card. At the checkout counters of several hundred supermarkets in the United States, no cash or checks need change hands. The clerk simply slips your plastic "debit" card into an electronic terminal connected by telephone line to the bank's computer, and the cost of your groceries is instantly transferred from your bank account to the store's.

Item: March 10, 1977   "Washington & Business: Postal Service and Electronic Transfer," *New York Times*

A panel of experts has advised the United States Postal Service to get involved quickly in electronic transmission of funds and messages, but so far they have received a cool reception from postal managers.

Item: March 25, 1977   "Monumental Legal Battle Shaping Up in Bid to Bar Color TV Recorders," *New York Times*

In a rapidly growing stack of briefs and affidavits at the Federal Court House here, a monumental legal battle is shaping up between the electronics industry and the entertainment industry. The stakes for both sides run into billions of dollars.

Item: March 29, 1977   "Memory Explosion: The Pocket Computer, Other Electronic Gear May Be Available Soon," *Wall Street Journal*

Electronics has come so far so fast that today's pocket calculators are nearly a match for yesterday's giant computers. Calculators weighing only a few ounces in many ways surpass the thirty-ton ENIAK, the first electronic digital computer built in 1946, and some devices rival computers of the 1950s.

Item: April 11, 1977   "The Imminent Videodisc Revolution," *Chronicle of Higher Education*

A 12-inch recording, in a system that will soon be marketed, can store—and reproduce on a home television set—enormous quantities of educational material—fifty-four thousand pages of text or graphic materials. The pages can be displayed one at a time on command or automatically at specified time intervals in forward or reverse order. The contents of the Encyclopaedia Brittanica could be stored on one disc.

AN ECONOMIC CHAIN REACTION

Elsewhere, Edwin B. Parker, taking into account the same kinds of reports, writes:

The strongest indication of changing demand for information services is the past and predicted expansion of the services made possible by . . . four technologies . . . [These are domestic satellites, video recording, expansion and diffusion of computer services, and cable television.] We seem to be in the midst of a chain reaction process (possibly the same one started by Gutenberg) in which information technology lowers the unit cost and increases the availability of information, generating more demand for information that sparks new advances in technology. The chain reaction process of new technology generating new demand is likely to continue for the foreseeable future. Although difficult to quantify, all indications are that information demand is the fastest growing in the economy with no leveling of demand in sight. The previous 'information explosion' and 'information input overload' problems resulting from having more information already available than we know how to process, have not resulted in any decrease in demand. Instead, they have generated a need for more individualized information channels and information filtering techniques, so that each individual can select what he wants or needs from the mass of information available in the society.[7]

ECONOMIC VIABILITY OF EXPANDED INFORMATION SYSTEMS

It doesn't seem to be a wild dream after all. The information society won't quit, or will it? We need to look more closely at the economic viability of expanded information systems.

The Economics of Information

Our understanding of the economics of information is imperfect despite a number of studies available. Information is not a standard commodity like all others, and our conventional economic indicators and analyses use models of the industrial society and, therefore, do not help very much to clarify the principal issues. We need to develop new models which will assist us to confirm, validate, and convince.

Future Investment in Information

We must also determine fairly soon the nature of efficient investment in information, and to decide who will provide the investment. The vexing social-policy questions of how much to invest in what kinds of information production and distribution remain, and of who will have access. There is a host of other questions and issues in need of resolution.

The Rodgers Report,[6] submitted to the Ford Administration in July of 1976 by the Domestic Council Committee on the Right of Privacy addresses itself to five "issue clusters":

   I. Government Information—Collection, Transfer and Dissemination

  II. Information in Commerce: A Resource for Public Good and Private Gain

 III. The Interaction Between Technology and Government

IV. International Implications of Information Policies and Developments

V. Preparing for the Information Age.

I recommend the Rodgers Report. It is clear and to the point, and has a good bibliography that will lead you to other studies. As you think about the issues, you may conclude that this must be what Alphonso X of Castile had in mind when he said, "If the Almighty had consulted me before embarking on the Creation, I should have recommended something simpler."

THE NEED FOR A NATIONAL INFORMATION POLICY

Who Will Make the Policy?

These are issues the outcome of which will affect the future of libraries, and all of us working in them. Leaders in business, government, and the voluntary sector will help to make the policies called for here. Society's pattern of handling information technology will be shaped by millions of decisions separately made but combined in their effects. The sum of the decisions will determine whether libraries will have a greater or lesser role in the information society. No one knows all of the answers, and you can safely assume that the board members of large telecommunications and computer organizations are scratching their heads just as we are doing.

Who Can Affect the Policy?

Individuals and professional organizations, libraries and information centers can all help to shape the policies. Major changes in banks, the post office, advertising, television, publishing, the telephone company, education, and libraries will not be accomplished without a lot of kicking and screaming and bitter rear-guard actions. Vested interests will fight the information society every inch of the way if they stand to lose economically and politically.

How can an individual deal with organizations and issues like these so deeply imbedded in institutional self interest? You start from where you are right now by adopting a personal coping strategy[19] along a scale from passive to active as you consider policies within your own library and library associations. Any position you take will affect the outcome.

Goals and the means of achieving them will be put forward by interested parties.

If you don't care about any of them, you may *retreat* by rejecting both goals and means.

If you don't want to make any waves, and are comfortable with the *status quo* as you now see it, you may *conform* by subscribing to the goals and means.

If you really don't like the goals, but want to give the appearance of supporting them, you will go through the motions of accepting the means. That's *conforming ritualistically.*

If you like the goals, but think the ways suggested for achieving them are all wrong, you may *innovate* by rejecting the means.

Finally, you may believe that the problem as now stated is an illusion, but rather than retreat you will decide to *rebel* and substitute a new set of goals and means of your own.

Retreating or conforming may make sense sometimes, but if we wish to have a useful and expanded role in the information society we'll need more innovators and rebels to debate the issues and to help formulate coordinated policies.

REFERENCES

1. Aronofsky, Julius S. and Robert R. Korfhage, "Telecommunication in Library Networks: A Five Year Projection," *Journal of Library Automation,* 10(1):16 (March 1977).
2. Baumol, William J. and Matityahu Marcus, *Economics of Academic Libraries.* Washington, DC: American Council on Education, 1973, p. 58.
3. Baumol, William J. and Janusz A. Ordover. "Public Good Properties in Reality: The Case of Scientific Journals." ASIS Proceedings, San Francisco, 1976. See also Baumol, William J. and William G. Bowen, *Performing Arts — The Economic Dilemma,* Chapter XVI, "On the Rationale of Public Support." New York: The Twentieth Century Fund, 1966.
4. Heilbroner, Robert L. "The False Promises of Growth," a review of *Social Limits to Growth* by Fred Hirsch. In *New York Review of Books,* (March 3, 1977).
5. Merton, Robert. *Perspectives on Organizations.* Washington, DC: American Association of Colleges for Teacher Education, 1976. [Adaptation of quote]
6. *National Information Policy.* Report to the President of the United States submitted by The Staff of the Domestic Council Committee on The Right of Privacy, Honorable Nelson A. Rockefeller, Chairman, Quincy Rodgers, Executive Director. Washington, DC: National Commission on Libraries and Information Science, 1976.
7. Parker, Edwin B. "Information and Society," in *Library and Information Service Needs of the Nation.* Proceedings of a Conference on the Needs of Occupational, Ethnic, and Other Groups in the United States. Washington, DC: National Commission on Libraries and Information Science, 1974, p. 36.
8. Parker, Edwin B. "Social Implications of Computer/Telecoms Systems," *Telecommunications Policy,* December 1976, p. 5.

9. Porat, Marc Uri. *The Information Economy.* Ann Arbor: Xerox University Microfilms, 1976, Vol. 1, Stanford University Ph.D. dissertation.
10. Ray, Gordon. "The Uses of the Past," paper presented at the Conference on Opportunities for Philanthropy. Bellagio, Italy, October 4-9, 1976.
11. Rosenblatt, Roger. "Information Science and Literary Scholarship," in "Views From The Modern Language Association Convention," by Margaret S. Jennings. *Bulletin of the American Society for Information Science.* 3(3) (February 1977).
12. Vickers, Geoffrey. *Freedom in a Rocking Boat: Changing Values in an Unstable Society.* Baltimore: Pelican Books, 1972.
13. Ways, Max. "Can Information Technology Be Managed?" in *Information Technology: Some Critical Implications for Decision Makers.* New York: The Conference Board, 1972.
14. Wiener, Norbert. *The Human Use of Human Beings.* New York: Avon Books, 1967.

The Impact of Economic Change on Libraries: A Review of the Literature

by William W. Sannwald

INTRODUCTION

During the last two decades, American libraries have experienced a period of economic growth and change that has exceeded any other period in their history. Ignited by the Russian space effort, American society re-examined its educational mission, and provided greater financial support to its schools and libraries.

This period of unquestioned growth for libraries slowed in the 1970s, as the United States faced new economic realities:

- Inflation, caused in part by the war in Asia, which made it impossible for libraries to retain their purchasing power.
- The end of cheap energy, signaled by the Arab oil embargo in 1973.
- Decay and decline in the central cities.
- A new concern for the environment that questioned the basic economic principles of America's marketing-oriented, consumption based economy.

These structural changes in the economy caused hardships for many libraries. A nation-wide reporting of the troubles affecting libraries is summarized in the *Wilson Library Bulletin*.[17] Morgan[36] relates the irony of budget cuts in public libraries, as use increases. De Gennaro[20] projects a new era of austerity for academic libraries, in which the financial resources available will not be enough to enable them to continue to build their collections and operate as they did in the past. He calls for librarians to shift emphasis away from holdings and size, to access and service. A similar call for cooperation and better management and planning in school media centers is expressed by Steepleton.[50]

Willison[58] lists the five major factors responsible for change in the American research libraries:
- Inflation of the costs of library materials, particularly serials and services.
- A decline in the real value of institutional endowments.
- A reduction in student enrollment and revenue fees.
- An alienation of traditional support for universities and research institutions.
- A drive toward unionization and participation in management among lower and middle professional staff in research libraries.

Bone[7] calls for the renewal of goals and objectives in public libraries in order to overcome crisis management. Priorities must be assigned if public libraries are to have a renaissance, and these priorities should have community input. Priorities assigned by Denver, Memphis and Detroit are discussed.

The purpose of this paper is to make a literature review of today's economic problems, and the responses being made to meet these challenges.

PRODUCTIVITY

Rohlf[46] states that libraries have a real productivity problem in relation to cost effectiveness. Rohlf tells of a university president who said that the library's budget is the toughest budget, because it is virtually a bottomless pit. No matter how much money is put into books and periodicals, librarians always need more. How are benefits quantified and when does an institution stop giving the library more money are questions that may not have answers.

Baumol and Marcus[5] contend that cost increases in libraries are a direct consequence of the amount of effort employed, and the range of library services that can be offered. Their study dispels the notion that inefficiency, or even inflation, can be blamed for increases in costs. Their analysis illustrates that rising cost trends are very much a matter of technology of library operations. As long as libraries adhere to traditional modes of operation, effective cost reduction is beyond their control.

It would be difficult to demonstrate that there has been a general upgrading of reference or information service at all commensurate with the improved technology available in public, academic and school libraries according to Galvin.[25] This is due to an orientation towards materials and not people on the part of librarians.

Atkinson[2] believes that computer systems have the potential for improving productivity. Almost all libraries have redundancy built into book selection, order, in-process, catalog, and circulation files. Enormous personnel savings could result if the same record could be carried through all the files, and be modified as it progresses through them.

Axford[3] states that today's budget crisis presents a golden opportunity for librarians to evaluate critically every system and procedure in terms of goals and priorities, and to weed out those that are obsolete. He illustrates productivity gains in the technical services area at Arizona State University by using performance measurement.

Reid[45] discusses practical ways that librarians are trying to improve productivity. Librarians are examining structural organization, work procedures, budgetary operations, and selection practices in order to become more cost efficient.

HUMAN RESOURCES

The manpower problem voiced most often in the early 1960s was where would the librarians be found to staff all the positions open in the nation's libraries. Probably most of these jobs did not really exist, and if they did, they had vanished by the mid 1970s.

Learmont and Darling[30] report that many library schools are having trouble placing their graduates. In their review of placements and salaries in 1975, they find that jobs are harder to find, many graduates are taking nonprofessional positions for a variety of reasons, and the number of positions being advertised widely may be decreasing. While salaries are higher, salary gains over previous years have not kept pace with inflation.

Even if salaries are not keeping up with inflation, salaries are still high enough to encourage alternatives to hiring Master's graduates. *Library Journal*[4] announces that the Baltimore County Public Library is using a Bachelor's training program to cut personnel costs. Savings of $2,000 per year are expected for each employee.

When a library has funds to hire employees, the actual process of hiring a new staff member may cost as much as $1,750, take twenty-six personnel action steps, and require six months of time according to Christofferson.[16]

UNIONISM

The economic impact of library unionism is expected to increase in the future. Bilbo traces early union activities, and Nyren[39] reports on the beginning of active organizing efforts in the 1960s.

The proceedings of the twentieth Allerton Park Institute[1] examined the state of library unionization today. The purpose of the institute was to present a thorough overview of the way collective bargaining actually functions in libraries today. Papers presented at the Institute were divided into three groups:

- General problems and current extent of library unionization.
- Specific, technical issues in the area of collective bargaining including the legal environment, recognition, bargaining units, scope of negotiations, grievances and disputes.

- Impact of collective bargaining in academic and public libraries.

Library Trends[15] for October 1976 is a good companion to the Allerton Papers because the issue was structured to avoid duplicating Allerton topics. Papers are divided into two sections:
- The first is concerned with the organizing process and its history. Included is how librarians perceive the advantages and disadvantages of unions; how librarians think of themselves as professionals, and the union's ability to represent professional interests; and the pros and cons of independent unions versus unions affiliated with other labor federations.
- The second section deals with the effects of collective bargaining—changes in the way employees and management view each other, as well as the effect of bargaining on the traditional managerial prerogatives.

LIBRARY MATERIALS

In most library budgets, the cost of library materials is the second largest item, exceeded only by staff salaries. During the last ten years, the cost of library materials has been increasing faster than the general inflation rate.

Monograph price increases have not been as rapid as serial increases. *Publishers Weekly*[55] reports that average prices increased by only one percent between 1975 and 1976—although there were major increases in fiction, art and biography. The average price of three major classes of books listed in fall announcement ads increased by approximately five percent per year during the period 1972-1976.

Increases in periodical prices during the period from 1967-1976 have averaged sixteen percent per year. According to Brown,[9] the average price of an American periodical increased from $8.66 in 1967, to $22.52 in 1976.

Clasquin[18] presents the dilemma caused by the rapid increase in serial costs. College and research libraries must allocate a greater portion of their funds for the maintenance of periodical collections rather than for monographs. Depending upon the institution and clientele served, serial costs may require as much as eighty percent of the reading materials budget.

De Gennaro[21] advises that many journals have virtually no individual subscribers, but are sold almost exclusively to libraries. He argues that many journals provide services primarily not to readers, but to the authors of the articles for whom publication brings professional recognition. This calls for action by librarians to weed titles, be more selective in their acquisition of new titles, and to engage in resource sharing. De Gennaro also suggests that librarians challenge and test the ethics and legality of differential subscription rates that allow publishers to charge libraries substantially more than individual subscribers.

A number of practical steps that librarians might take to stretch their materials funds are expressed by Burton.[11] Included are the use of formula budgeting, establishing priorities of collecting by building on strengths, delaying perhaps indefinitely retrospective purchases, developing clear policies on interdisciplinary programs, and having book sales to sell duplicates.

Little[32] relates the experience of the Oklahoma County Libraries System's trailer bookmobiles, which converted their collections from hardbound to paperback books. Fines were also eliminated and books were arranged by topical categories. After the change, circulation increased and costs of materials were lowered.

LIBRARY COOPERATION

Partnership and cooperation among libraries is not new, but the formal agreements and shared services taking place today will probably increase, causing many changes in library operations.

Stuart-Stubbs[51] gives an historical review of resource sharing during the late nineteenth and early twentieth centuries that sets the scene for the cooperative activities of today and tomorrow.

Library cooperation is the theme of the October 1975 issue of *Library Trends*.[27] Included are papers dealing with:

- An historical review of cooperative activities showing common elements, and an optimistic forecast of future growth.
- Consequences of external political and technological factors.
- Need for legal contracts in future efforts.
- Statistical information needed to plan cooperatives, and the merits of cooperation.
- Cooperation at the regional, state, and federal levels, as well as cooperation outside of the United States.

Nyren's "Skirmish Line"[38] presents concerns of cooperation as seen by a variety of librarians. Concerns cover the range from the large library that fears its resources will be exhausted, to the smaller library that must decide what network services it will acquire.

Ferguson[22] examines contemporary resource sharing at both the national and regional level. He feels that planning should take place at both levels, and that sufficient controls must exist so that the needs of regional groups are not disregarded in efforts to build national networks.

ENERGY

Library Journal[37] reports that many libraries were forced to shut down as a result of the natural gas shortage in the winter of 1976-1977. The Minneapolis Public Library cut its hours of service, and the Free Library of Philadelphia closed forty branches heated by natural gas.

Philadelphia's main library and seven branches built in recent years were kept open because they were not heated by gas. Library Director, Keith Doms, said they saw the energy crisis coming and did not want to be dependent on gas.

The proceedings of the 1974 Library Architecture Preconference Institute[31] conclude that most of the designs submitted do not use energy saving measures. If energy savings were employed in building design, long-term cost savings would occur.

Tinglum[53] responds to the need for energy conservation with some operational practices savings. Most of the savings recommended concern lighting management.

Air conditioning in a properly designed library is not wasteful of energy according to Torrance.[54] Lighting standards reflecting energy conservation are advanced by the Illuminating Engineering Society.[28]

Use of solar energy[48] was pioneered at the Troy-Miami Public Library with the building designed to use a solar system to supply 77% of the heating requirements. The solar system will also cool the building, and energy savings are expected to total $2,900 for the 23,200 square foot building. Solar energy will also be used in the new 60,000 square foot New Rochelle building.[40] The plant will provide 42% of the heat, 17% of the cooling, and 83% of the hot water needed by the library.

TECHNOLOGY

Baumol and Marcus[5] argue that the rising costs of library operations emanate from the technological structure of library operations—that is, their labor intensity. The use of data processing has proceeded far less rapidly because the electronic systems have proven less flexible and useful than was originally claimed, because of the complexity of library operations, the resistance to innovation by librarians, and the high cost and rapid obsolesence of equipment. They point out that the long-run cost savings of electronic operations in libraries will mean significant savings because labor costs will price conventional methods out of existence.

Technology of the Ohio College Library Center (OCLC) has probably been the most significant development to change the structure of library operations. Plotnik[13] provides an overview of OCLC and its impact on libraries. *Library Technology Reports*[35] gives a thorough background of OCLC and the benefits and limitations of the system.

Veaner[56] describes BALLOTS, an alternative network to OCLC. Currently there are more than eighty libraries that use BALLOTS and further expansion is expected as unit costs of operation drop.

Database vendors[19] of on-line services have begun to drop prices as competition increases in the library market place. The question of how low prices will drop is not known, but use is expected to increase as unit costs decline.

Online circulation costs[42] are also expected to decrease as more vendors enter the market. The Suburban Library System in Illinois estimates their circulation costs for the CLSI system average $750 per month to a library circulating 8,750 items per month.

Brownrigg and Bruer[10] tell some of the problems, issues, and alternatives in designing individual, stand-alone systems for servicing library operations, and analyze potential problems when these minisystems are later connected with a larger network.

Folcarelli and Ferragamo[23] describe the potential economic savings and operational advantages of microforms.

FUNDING SOURCES

Library Trends[13] of July 1975 recounts the history, future, and impact of federal aid to libraries. Federal aid has caused expansion of library services in the past and will play a significant role in the future. Included in the issues are:

- A legislative history of LSA and LSCA, and the changes it has made in library service.
- A history and study of the effects of Title II of the Elementary and Secondary Education Act.
- The impact on academic libraries of Title II-A of the Higher Education Act.
- A summary of federal funding for library education and research.
- The role of ALA in library legislation.

The recognition of the obligation of a state to fund a local library that serves users beyond its municipal borders[49] is illustrated by Michigan's funding of the Detroit Public Library. The Enoch Pratt Library[52] urged a large increase in state aid for serving as a state resource in Maryland.

An argument against federal programs for libraries is advanced by O'Halloran.[41] He feels that libraries could be better funded through changes in the tax law so that credit against income tax payment may be taken for gifts to libraries. With this tax incentive, librarians and others who realize the desperate financial needs of libraries could do something about it and witness the results. This would eliminate fund administration by federal and state bureaucracies.

Fees to provide information and reference service in tax supported libraries is questioned by Berry.[6] The outcome of this problem is still undecided.

BUDGETING TECHNIQUES

Wedgeworth[57] explores some of the major dimensions of budgeting in school media centers, and takes a look at the nature of the budgeting process including Program, Planning and Budgeting Systems (PPBS). McCauley[33] gives a procedural guide to PPBS and relates that since the advent of PPBS and the transformation of school libraries to school media centers, librarians have become deeply and time-consumingly involved in budgeting. McCauley also reviews valid sources of funding for school media centers.

Burton[12] examines various approaches used in formula budgeting and presents a new technique developed for the University of Michigan. Burton's formula projects book fund needs, as well as staffing needs in public services, technical services and administration. The formula is related to the concept of the weighted user, where quantitative measures are applied to users of the library at different levels of sophistication.

Techniques to allocate book budgets are presented by McGrath, Kohut and Gold:

- McGrath[31] proposes a statistical technique to allocate book funds based on the purpose of the book collection and demand of users.
- Kohut[29] advances a model for balancing the purchase of serials against the purchase of monographs by using individual funding units within the academic library.
- Gold[26] criticizes Kohut's model because he says it ignores considerations of economic efficiency. Gold proposes a micro-economic model for serials-monograph allocations that uses marginal cost, marginal benefit analysis.

Cost benefit analysis for determining public library budgets is presented by Francis[24] who develops a correlation matrix from statistics dealing with population, library expenditures, and circulation.

Zero-based budgeting is the latest technique to be used by librarians. Pyhrr[44] who helped implement the system that Jimmy Carter used in Georgia, has written the classic text on the subject. *Library Journal*[39] reports on seminars dealing with zero-based budgeting for librarians.

It is apparent that a variety of economic forces are at work to affect the operations of all libraries, and no clear solutions are immediately apparent. The next years will no doubt see mounting financial problems, and greater attention must be given to solving them.

REFERENCES

1. Allerton Park Institute. 20th, 1974. "Collective Bargaining in Libraries," (proceeding of a conference sponsored by the Illinois State Library, the University of Illinois Graduate School of Library Science, and the University of Illinois Office of Continuing Education and Public Service) ed. by Frederick A. Schleph. Urbana-Champaign: University of Illinois Graduate School of Library Science, 1975.

2. Atkinson, Hugh C. "Personnel Savings Through Computerized Library Systems," *Library Trends* 23:587-94 (April 1975).
3. Axford, H. William. "Performance Measurement Revisited," *College and Research Libraries* 34:249-57 (September 1973).
4. "Bachelor's Replacing M.L.S.," *Library Journal* 102:862 (April 15, 1977).
5. Baumol, William J. and Marcus, Matityahu. *Economics of Academic Libraries*. Washington, DC: American Council on Education, 1973.
6. Berry, John. "The Fee Dilemma," *Library Journal* 102:651 (March 15, 1977).
7. Bone, Larry Earl. "The Public Library Goals and Objectives Movement: Death Gasp or Renaissance?" *Library Journal* 100:1283-6 (July 1975).
8. Breivik, Patricia Senn. "Foundation Funding," *Library Journal* 100:2298-2302 (December 15, 1975).
9. Brown, Norman B. "Price Indexes for '76: U.S. Periodicals and Serial Services," *Library Journal* 101:1600-5 (August, 1976).
10. Brownrigg, Edwin Blake and Bruer, J. Michael. "Automated Turn-Key Systems in the Library: Prospects and Perils," *Library Trends* 14:727-36 (April, 1976).
11. Burton, Robert E. "Book Selection and Budget Cuts in Academic Libraries," *Michigan Libraries* 41:7-9 (Spring 1975).
12. Burton, Robert E. "Formula Budgeting: An Example," *Special Libraries* 66:61-7 (February 1975).
13. Casey, Genevieve M., ed. "Federal Aid to Libraries: Its History, Impact, Future," *Library Trends* 24:1-153 (July 1975).
14. Chapin, Richard E. "Library Consortia: Why?" *Catholic Library World* 46:326-8 (March 1975).
15. Chaplan, Margaret A., ed. "Employee Organizations and Collective Bargaining in Libraries," *Library Trends* 25:419-557 (October 1976).
16. Christofferson, Rea. "The High Cost of Hiring," *Library Journal* 102:677-81 (March 15, 1977).
17. "The Cities and the Suburbs: A Look at Library $$ in Hard Times," *Wilson Library Bulletin* 50:292-293 (December 1975).
18. Clasquin, F.F. "Serials: Costs and Budget Projections," *Drexel Library Quarterly* 11:64-71 (July 1975).
19. "Database Vendors in a Price War?" *Library Journal* 102:665 (March 15, 1977).

20. De Gennaro, Richard. "Austerity, Technology, and Resource Sharing: Research Libraries Face the Future," *Library Journal* 100:917-23 (May 15, 1975).

21. De Gennaro, Richard. "Escalating Journal Prices: Time to Fight Back," *American Libraries* 8:69-74 (February 1977).

22. Ferguson, Douglas. "Nation Wide Resource Sharing: Visions and Assessment," *California Librarian* 36:49-55 (April 1975).

23. Folcarelli, Ralph J. and Ferragamo, Ralph C. "Microform Publications: Hardware and Suppliers," *Library Trends* 24:711-25 (April 1976).

24. Francis, D. Pitt. "Cost Benefit Analysis and Public Library Budgets," *Library Review* 25:189-92 (Spring, Summer 1976).

25. Galvin, Thomas J. "The Education of the New Reference Librarian," *Library Journal* 100:727-30 (April 15, 1975).

26. Gold, Steven D. "Allocating the Book Budget: An Economic Model," *College and Research Libraries* 36:397-402 (Summer 1975).

27. Grove, Pearce S., ed. "Library Cooperation," *Library Trends* 24:157-423 (October 1975).

28. Illuminating Engineering Society. Subcommittee on Library Lighting. "Recommended Practice of Library Lighting; an IES Transaction," *Journal of the Illuminating Engineering Society* 3:253-66 (April 1974).

29. Kohut, Joseph J. "Allocating the Book Budget: A Model." *College and Research Libraries* 35:192-9 (May 1974).

30. Learmont, Carol L. and Darling, Richard L. "Placements and Salaries 1975: A Difficult Year," *Library Journal* 101:1487-93 (July 1976).

31. Library Architecture Preconference Institute, New York, 1974. "An Architectural Strategy for Change: Remodeling and Expanding for Contemporary Public Library Needs; Proceeding." ed. by Raymond M. Holt. Chicago: American Library Association, 1976.

32. Little, Paul. "Le$$ Costly, More Popular," *Library Journal* 102:451-6 (February 15, 1977).

33. McCauley, Elfrieda. "Budgeting for School Media Services," *School Media Quarterly* 4:126-34 (Winter 1976).

34. McGrath, William E. "A Pragmatic Book Allocation Formula for Academic and Public Libraries with a Test for its Effectiveness," *Library Resources and Technical Services* 19:356-69 (Fall 1975).

35. Markuson, Barbara Evans. "The OCLC Online Network: The Top Management View. Part II of the Ohio College Library Center System," *Library Technology Reports* 12:40-65 (January 1976).
36. Morgan, Jane Hale. "Dwindling Economy—Booming Library Use," *Michigan Librarian* 41:12-3 (Spring 1975).
37. "1977's Energy Crunch: Libraries Shut Down," *Library Journal* 102:666 (March 15, 1977).
38. Nyren, Karl E. "Investing in Network Services: How Far Can We Go?" [Interviews.] *Library Journal* 101:1394-6 (June 15, 1976).
39. Nyren, Karl. "Libraries and Labor Unions," *Library Journal* 92:2115-21 (June 1, 1967).
40. Nyren, Karl. "Solar Energy for New Rochelle Library." *LJ/SLJ Hotline* 6:6 (May 23, 1977).
41. O'Halloran, Charles. "I, for One, Wish that There Were No Federal Programs for Libraries," *American Libraries* 6:290-2 (May 1975).
42. "Online Circulation Costs Pegged," *Library Journal* 102:867 (April 15, 1977).
43. Plotnik, Art. "OCLC for You—and Me?!: A Humanized Anatomy for Beginners," *American Libraries* 7:257-75 (May 1976).
44. Pyhrr, Peter A. *Zero-based Budgeting: A Practical Management Tool for Evaluating Expenses.* New York: Wiley, 1973.
45. Reid, Marion T. "Coping with Budget Adversity: The Impact of the Financial Squeeze on Acquisitions," *College and Research Libraries* 37:266-72 (May 1976).
46. Rohlf, Robert H. "Library Costs and Budgets," *Minnesota Libraries* 24:39-45 (Summer 1973).
47. Scannell, Francis X. "The Present Economic Crisis and Libraries," *Michigan Librarian* 41:5 (Spring 1975).
48. "Solar Nexus: Library Pioneers in Tapping the Sun's Energy," *American Libraries* 8:188-90 (April 1977).
49. "State Takes Over Funding for Detroit Public Library," *Library Journal* 101:1578-1979 (August 1976).
50. Steepleton, Judith. "Facing Reality: The '75-'76 School Year," *Michigan Librarian* 41:9-10 (Spring 1975).
51. Stuart-Stubbs, Basil. "An Historical Look at Resource Sharing," *Library Trends* 23:649-64 (April 1975).
52. "Substantial State Aid to Enoch Pratt Urged," *Library Journal* 102:316-9 (February 1, 1977).
53. Tinglum, John H. "Saving Energy Is Today's Game! Heat, Cool, Ventilate and Light With Care," *Wisconsin Library Bulletin* 71:207-8 (September-October 1975).

54. Torrance, J.S. "A Justification of Air Conditioning in Libraries," *Journal of Librarianship* 7:199-206 (July 1975).
55. "U.S. Book Industry Statistics: Prices, Sales, Trends," *Publishers Weekly* 211:52-6 (February 14, 1977).
56. Veaner, Allen B. "BALLOTS—The View from Technical Services," *Library Resources and Technical Services* 21:127-46 (Spring 1977).
57. Wedgeworth, Robert. "Budgeting for School Media Centers," *School Libraries* 20:29-35 (Spring 1971).
58. Willison, I.R. "The American Research Library System in a Period of Constraint: Some Impressions," *Journal of American Studies* 9:21-34 (April 1975).
59. "Zero-Based Budgeting Meets; Carter Explains Policy," *Library Journal* 102:437-8 (February 15, 1977).

The New Role of the Librarian in the Information Age

by Gerald R. Shields

I think we had better charge a dollar for admission to the library to keep the crowds in check. We should also charge, naturally, for the coffee and Danish in the scattered coffee rooms, and for the records played in the sound rooms, and for the films, and for time at any of the computer consoles, and a slight reservation fee for assuring the availability of any of the small meeting rooms, and for lunches in the cafeteria, and for typewriters, telephone calls, reproduction, etc. But I am against charging for strolls through the art collections or the gardens, or for extensive reference services, or the guided tours, or the introductions to the use of various equipment, or for the use of the books on the premises, or for listening to the day's roster of interesting lectures and video programs, or for the use of the rest rooms, or for occasional use of the infant-care and day-care facilities.

Libraries, properly conceived, make a lot more sense than colleges, improperly conceived. If they are to take over the useful functions of a college, I guess we will have to add a gymnasium and a beer garden and a notary public to certify testing results.[1]

ROLE OF THE LIBRARIAN

What is the role of the librarian in a technological society where information is an infinite national resource while the physical resources are finite? What is the role of the librarian in a technological society where change is dependent upon swift and knowledgeable policy and decision-making? What is required from the librarian when the technology of information is accelerating social change to a level wherein we wonder if we are losing control? The fast-paced change and the demand for responsible decision-making has created a feeling of helplessness, frustration, doubt and fear because the utilization of information technology has not kept pace with its availability. Where and what is the role of the librarian in this social condition?

The librarian should be acting as an information transfer agent. The librarian must be allowed to fulfill an advocacy role in the utilization of information technology. If information is our infinite resource, then the ability to utilize the finite physical resources most assuredly depends upon information technology and the librarian.

EFFECT OF INFORMATION TECHNOLOGY ON EDUCATION

There is another way to approach this concept. Instead of looking the information technology monster in the eye, look instead at the effect upon education. Marvin Adelson has said that:

> The changeability of the environment and the enormous growing mass of knowledge are leading to a shift in emphasis away from attempting to learn what is known in anticipation of its possible later value, toward learning the means of finding out what one has to know when the need arises.[1]

Think about that for a moment. Relate to the manner in which most of us "got our learnin'." We were taught to fill up the computer in our head with data. We crammed as much as we could into it. We memorized facts, figures, dates, historical trends, and civilization ends. Then, yellow pencil in hand, we tested ourselves by trying to retrieve the information from our brain. Our life and future depended upon those exercises.

If we go along with Adelson then we must recognize that it is becoming ever more important to be able to locate what it is you need to know than it is to gather data into the mind for possible future use. That data gathering is a wasteful practice, for some of the data stored up may never be used or constantly have to be reshuffled into a life-long pattern of data collecting better known as continuing education.

KINGDOMS OF INFORMATION OWNERS

The significance of that concept cannot be lost upon librarians who have traditionally been functioning as information transfer agents. Librarians have gathered up the data, stored it and waited for someone to come along who wanted to know. Today we are faced with a society dependent upon its technology. We are faced with a technology which thrives on acceleration. And with that acceleration goes social change. And if society cannot find the information it needs to know to meet the accelerated pace of decision-making, then technology becomes destructive rather than constructive. And in a destructive society, information falls into the hands of a few. Instead of baronies of landowners, we could face kingdoms of information owners.

In a report from the U.S. Department of Agriculture in 1968, the author Lester R. Brown reported that "of the 50 largest economic entities [in the world], 37 are countries and 13 are corporations. Of the top 100, 51 are corporations."[2] It is obvious from those statistics that the world order is changing. And that change is accelerating with the utilization of information technology. Where is the librarian in this political entity? You know the answer. They are the information transfer agents. The information transfer agent with a country or a corporation as a client. The survival of the client will depend on the ability of the information transfer agent to utilize information technology.

That is fine for the country or the corporation, but what about people in those economic entities? Where is their fiefdom of information? If they need to know how to find what they need to know, where will they learn? Will the individual as a child begin by discovering that information can be found in a variety of places, in a variety of ways? Will the child grow by learning simple computer languages and retrieval processes? Upon reaching adulthood, will they know *where* to go and *how* to find what they need to know in order to survive? Who is the librarian for this individual entity? You know the answer. The librarian is the information transfer agent. Librarians are the information transfer agents with the individual as a client. The survival of the client will be dependent upon the ability of the information transfer agent to utilize information technology.

It would seem that Robert M. Hayes was right a couple of years ago when he said, "It may well be that the role of the librarian is not changing as much as we think it is.[3] We are still needed as acquisitioners, catalogers, and communicators of data packages.

Paul Wasserman does not wholly accept this constricted view of the librarian. He said in his book,

> The problems of the times and the problems of the institution require those of spirit and action, who are fired by a vision not of what the institutions and professional practice now are, but what they can become. A new pioneering class not constrained or disabled by conventions of the field is needed, one who perceives the challenge and the opportunity of the institution and of the information form.[4]

What is the challenge of the information form? The challenge to the individual is vital. The technology of information can be used to create, but it can also be used to control the desire for social change. There are dangers to the individual in the technological society of information overload, invasion of privacy, manipulation to control news and mold opinion, increased surveillance and monitoring "in the public interest," a decrease in social cohesion with greater fragmentation of attitude and motivation, and certainly, increased discrimination via inequitable access to advanced skills necessary to use information effectively. Therein is the challenge. Information is the tool which determines the extent of freedom for the individual in the development of their full potential. Information determines the freedom with which such social agencies as government, law, education, commerce, labor, industry, etc. are able to function. And information is the tool for freedom in the agencies developed to collect information so that it may be retrieved for the use of all the society.

OPPORTUNITIES AND BENEFITS IN INFORMATION TECHNOLOGY

This pioneering class of librarians Dr. Wasserman calls for will meet not only challenge, but they will find opportunities and benefits in information technology. The laws and ethics necessary to profitably operate this technology are only beginning to form and librarians must participate in that formulation. Necessary decisions must be made to insure that information technology is a creative force in the pursuit of social justice in our society. And the librarian as a professional must meet the challenge first by realizing that professional goals and objectives are not to be fragmented by type-of-institution. Instead, the goals and objectives of all librarians should be united into a common purpose by type-of-service. The quality of service in academic and research levels is directly dependent upon the quality of service in the school and public libraries because the quality of life for all ages in this technological society is dependent on the ability of the individual to be able to *find* what it is one needs to know throughout one's lifetime.

And information technology offers even a broader range of opportunity for the librarian. The technology already has opened the sensory ranges available to the individual, thus enhancing the aesthetics of living (have you heard quadraphonic sound or seen a holograph?). The technology enables the librarian to provide highly personalized information and communications exchange (ever had a database produce a bibliography just for you?). And through technology the professional librarian will be called upon to develop their interpersonal skills in order to help the user of information develop full potential, make more free and voluntary choices, and enhance their levels of knowing, caring, and achieving.

The role of the librarian in the new technological age is in reality the old role as it has been perceived but in reality not often achieved. Because the librarian has resisted change and has been content to hide behind the circulation, catalog or reference desk rather than make that proud and responsible step out into the social arena where we all are threatened by the accelerated changes going on about us. Those who cannot step up to the challenge of serving people through the utilization of technological developments in the delivery of user-oriented information will have to step aside. We have a lot to learn and we have a long way to go if we are to provide information services to insure the people's opportunity to participate, to learn, to achieve self-fulfillment, to pursue careers, and to maintain dignity and tranquility. If we cannot accept our common purpose as professionals, society will pass us by and we will witness the creation of authoritarian structures which through control of information would threaten and possibly destroy the free society we seek to build.

REFERENCES

1. Adelson, Marvin. "Education: At the Crossroads of Decision," in *Information Technology*. Clearing House, 1972. p. 112-7.

2. Brown, Lester R. *The Nation State, The Multinational Corporation and the Changing World Order.* Washington, DC: U.S. Department of Agriculture, 1968.
3. Hayes, Robert M. "The Changing Role of the Librarian," *Journal of Chemical Documentation* 14(3):118-20 (1974).
4. Wasserman, Paul. *The New Librarianship: A Challenge for Change.* New York: Bowker, 1972. p. 274.

The New Role of Librarians as Professionals: A Literature Review

by Thomas J. Galvin, Barbara Immroth,
Margaret Mary Kimmel,
Desretta V. McAllister, and
James M. Matarazzo

In "Professionalism Reconsidered,"[7] Bundy and Wasserman suggest that redefinition of three major relationships—with clients, with institutions, and with professional groups—is central to the advancement of librarianship. Their discussion of professional attitudes, practices, and responsibilities delineates problems still unresolved and provides a natural framework for consideration of the new role of librarians as professionals.

RELATIONSHIPS WITH CLIENTS

As librarians shift their emphasis to a more client-centered approach, the needs of individuals become pivotal to the services provided by staff and to the content and character of collections. Several public libraries have experimented with this approach. For example, the adult learner was the focus of a special project which incorporated the efforts of four libraries with the College Level Examination Board.[25] The most fully documented and extensive adult learning experiment was conducted by the Dallas Public Library with the cooperation of Southern Methodist University.[6] Penland has sought to provide a general model for this new role of librarian as learning consultant.[27]

Public libraries, in what appears to be a continuing search for new directions, are engaged in a series of local experiments, especially in the area of information and referral service. A recent issue of the *Drexel Library Quarterly*[5] is devoted to an attempt to build a theoretical base for library I & R services, noting the absence of total institutional commitment as one of the critical factors restricting the growth of the service. Childers[10] extends the discussion to the Neighborhood Information Center Project, analyzing the future of I & R services in the public library and stressing the need for research. On the other hand, the failure of such an experiment at the Enoch Pratt Free Library is chronicled by Donahue.[13,14] Robbins[30] cautions, however, that while new services are planned for clients and new directions are posited for the public library, citizen participation remains minimal in library planning or policy making.

As early as 1963, Freiser[17] urged a reorientation of school library services toward information delivery to students. More recent efforts to focus competencies of the school media specialist[8] on needs of the learner have been defined by the publication of new standards.[2] A reemphasis on the role of reading guidance is the result of the renewed priority given to reading in many school districts.[3,28] At the same time, both Wood[32] and Chisholm[11] note the necessity of the media specialist's involvement in curriculum design.

Smith[33] suggests that this role in curriculum design is essential to the college and university library as well. Programs like those developed at Monteith, Federal City and Mankato Colleges, among others[23] continue to focus on integrating the learning experience of the individual with the total library program.

RELATIONSHIPS WITH INSTITUTIONS

Our assumption is that any new role either thrust upon or entered into eagerly by librarians will be affected by the three relationships mentioned by Bundy and Wasserman. The second of these—with the institution—has been the subject of much discussion. Galvin,[18] while commenting on the rampant survivalist attitudes of librarians and institutions, reminds us "that institutional change is both inevitable and desirable." In order to face these changes, he proposes that library managers "devise and implement sound methods for establishing realistic, achievable, appropriate service goals." In two articles, Downs[15,26] argues convincingly for academic library directors with flexibility and adaptability in order to survive whatever changes are forced upon them.

One of the changes most likely to alter libraries markedly is the renewed interest in implementing the concept of resource sharing. At a recent Pittsburgh conference,[21] nationally known library leaders offered their perceptions of the problems and promises of sharing. The question seems to be not whether libraries will share, but how, and to what degree, and with whom.

The special librarian, too, will have to adapt to institutional expectations according to both Ladendorf[24] and Echelman.[16] This will require librarians to extend their services while developing expertise with the new technologies and the management of information.

Recent data, however, continues to support the view that most special libraries, particularly within the corporate sector, are typically one and two person operations.

A Strategy for Public Library Change: Proposed Public Library Goals[25] offers an important statement for libraries seeking to enhance their impact on clients, though presenting no simple solutions to the public library in its quest for new directions. The 1975 PLA "Goals and Guidelines for Community Library Service"[20] reflects a similar thrust toward institutional change. The persistent theme of the need for research is reiterated in an issue of *Library Trends*[4] devoted to community analysis. Articles reflect the application of community and/or user studies as instruments for planning.

Automation has affected many aspects of the institutions where librarians work, and certainly the library has been influenced and changed by this and other new technologies. De Gennaro[12] reviews these areas and presents an overview of the impact of technology on libraries. Galvin[19] has suggested that the new electronic and computer technologies have developed more rapidly than our capacity or will to make effective use of them to provide enhanced service to clients.

RELATIONSHIPS WITH THE PROFESSION

The librarian of the future will be dealing with the pressures of a diminished job market calling for more carefully honed and specialized job skills and career planning. A Bureau of Labor Statistics study[34] of supply and demand for library manpower through 1975 predicts a slowing in the growth of employment, a modest demand for replacement librarians, and a strong demand for minority librarians as well as selected specializations.

Kingsbury's[22] study anticipates the further specialization of school media specialists while noting a continuing emphasis on the librarian as curriculum consultant. School librarians have gone beyond forecasting a changed role to actively shaping new careers as developed in the School Library Manpower Project.[9]

Surely the role of the librarian will be influenced by the training of those who enter the profession in the future. The 1972 Standards for Accreditation[1,35] provide many insights into the education of those who will join the profession.

A final caution is offered by Jesse H. Shera:

> We cannot afford to rest on such laurels as we may have. We must face the unpleasant fact that, except for some rather dramatic advances in our professional technology, librarianship is basically much the same as it was in the days of Dewey, Cutter, Bowker and their contemporaries. But theirs was a relatively complacent and comfortable world. Today, in our race against disaster, we are . . . losing our lead time, and mankind does stand at the crossroads.[31]

REFERENCES

1. American Library Association, Committee on Accreditation. *Standards for Accreditation.* Chicago: American Library Association, 1972.
2. American Association of School Librarians, American Library Association, and Association for Educational Communication and Technology. *Media Programs: District and School.* Chicago: American Library Association, 1975.
3. Beckermann, E. P. "Woodbridge Tutorial Program," *School Library Journal* 22:22-5 (February 1976).
4. Bone, Larry Earl. "Community Analysis and Libraries," ed. *Library Trends* 24 (January 1976).
5. Braverman, Miriam, ed. "Information and Referral Services in the Public Library," *Drexel Library Quarterly* 12 (January-April, 1976).
6. Brooks, Jean S. and Reich, David L. *The Public Library in Nontraditional Education.* Homewood, IL: ETC, 1974.
7. Bundy, Mary Lee and Wasserman, Paul. "Professionalism Reconsidered," *College and Research Libraries* 29:5-26 (January 1968).
8. Case, Robert N. and Lowrey, Anna Mary. *Behavioral Requirements Analysis Checklist (BRAC): A Compilation of Competency-based Job Functions and Task Statements for School Library Media Personnel; Phase II: School Library Manpower Project.* Chicago: American Library Association, 1973.
9. School Library Manpower Project. *Curriculum Alternatives: Experiments in School Library Media Education,* by Case, Robert N. and Lowrey, Anna Mary. Chicago: American Library Association, 1974.
10. Childers, Thomas. "The Neighborhood Information Center Project," *Library Quarterly* 46:271-89 (July 1976).
11. Chisholm, Margaret E. and Ely, Donald P. *Media Personnel in Education: A Competency Approach.* Englewood Cliffs, NJ: Prentice Hall, 1976.
12. De Gennaro, Richard. "Library Automation: Changing Patterns and New Directions," *Library Journal* 101:175-83 (January 1, 1976).
13. Donohue, Joseph. "Planning for a Community Information Center," *Library Journal* 97:3284-8 (October 15, 1972).
14. Donohue, Joseph. "Some Experiments Fail: The Public Information Center Project at the Enoch Pratt Free Library," *Library Journal* 100:1185-90 (June 15, 1975).
15. Downs, Robert B. "The Role of the Academic Librarian, 1876-1976," *College and Research Libraries* 37:491-501 (November 1976).

16. Echelman, Shirley. "Toward the New Special Library," *Library Journal* 101:91-4 (January 1, 1976).
17. Freiser, L. H. "Information Retrieval for Students," *Library Journal* 88:1121-3 (March 15, 1963).
18. Galvin, Thomas J. "Beyond Survival: Library Management for the Future," *Library Journal* 101:1833-5 (September 15, 1976).
19. Galvin, Thomas J. "The Education of the New Reference Librarian," *Library Journal* 106:727-30 (April 15, 1975).
20. "Goals and Guidelines for Community Library Service," *PLA Newsletter* 14:9-13 (June 1975).
21. Kent, Allen and Galvin, Thomas J., eds. *Library Resource Sharing.* New York: Marcel Dekker, 1977.
22. Kingsbury, Mary E. "Education for School Librarianship: Expectation vs. Reality," *Journal of Education for Librarianship* 15:251-7 (Spring 1975).
23. Knapp, Patricia B. "Involving the Library in an Integrated Learning Environment," in *Libraries and the College Climate of Learning.* Syracuse: Syracuse University Press, 1964; and *Monteith College Library Experiment.* Metuchen, NJ: Scarecrow Press, 1966.
24. Ladendorf, Janice M. "The Special Librarian in the Modern World," *Special Libraries* 61:531-7 (December 1970).
25. Mavor, Anne S., Toro, Jose O., and DeProspo, Ernest R. *Role of Public Libraries in Independent Learning; Parts I & II.* New York: College Entrance Examination Board, 1976.
26. McAnally, Arthur M. and Downs, Robert B. "The Changing Role of Directors of University Libraries," *College and Research Libraries* 34:103-25 (March 1973).
27. Penland, Patrick R. *Librarian as Learning Consultant.* Pittsburgh: University of Pittsburgh Book Center, 1976.
28. Portteus, Eleanor M. "Cleveland's Media Centers Go All Out for Reading," *Wilson Library Bulletin* 50:725-7 (May 1976).
29. Public Library Association. *A Strategy for Public Library Change: Proposed Public Library Goals—Feasibility Study.* Allie Beth Martin, Project Coordinator. Chicago: American Library Association, 1972.
30. Robbins, Jane. *Citizen Participation and Public Library Policy.* Metuchen, NJ: Scarecrow Press, 1975.
31. Shera, Jesse H. "Failure and Success: Assessing a Century," *Library Journal* (January 1, 1976). pp. 281-7.
32. "SLJ Symposium: Personalizing Library Services for Children and Young Adults," *School Library Journal* 21:67-71 (March 1975).

33. Smith, Jessie C. "Library Inter-com: A New Approach," *South Carolina Librarian* 16:27-32 (Spring 1972).
34. United States Bureau of Labor Statistics. *Library Manpower: A Study of Demand and Supply.* Washington, DC: U.S. Government Printing Office, 1975.
35. Veaner, Allen B. "The Anatomy of Accreditation," *American Libraries* 6:552-4 (October 1975).

Public Access To Information in the Post-Industrial Society

by Fay M. Blake

First of all, let me tell you a fairy tale, a very modern fairy tale. It was written by a captain of industry (or of post-industry?), Howard J. Hilton, of Hilmark United Corporation, and he calls it "An Ideal Information Access System." I'll just read you one paragraph:

> The technical requirements [of this ideal information access system] include both the hardware and the software necessary to meet the varied needs of both the users and the producers of knowledge and information. The users require hardware that is capable of providing access through all available media. It should cover the full range of cost and benefit, from the simplest and least expensive to the most sophisticated, providing a central store and backup for the individual systems supporting local users throughout the world. With present hardware, the sophisticated system would have time-shared terminals linked by broad band satellite communications to major computer centers throughout the world; optical readers for high reduction microforms; cathode ray tubes (CRT) with high resolution capability; buffered storage for static alphanumeric and graphic material; switching capability for audio, video, and television reception at distant stations; an optical computer for conducting Boolean searches and reading binary data into the main computer at nanosecond rates; and microfiche and hardcopy print capability from both the optical reader and the CRT. For the near future, the most sophisticated system may be a combination of the laser and holographic technology. And beyond that, who can guess what the future holds?[6]

TIME OUT FOR FAIRY TALES

Once upon a time, when I was more vitally interested in fairy tales than I am now, it was all a lot simpler. A girl kissed a frog and, presto, he turned into a prince and everyone lived happily ever after. Now, if this monstrous dream of Hilton's is the ideal information access system, for whom is it ideal? Let me tell you parts of another story. In 1965 the Cleveland Public Library began an experimental project for "limited readers." That's a euphemism for illiterate adults and there are 50,000 of them in Cleveland, and about eleven million in the United States, and the figure is rising, not diminishing. The Cleveland

Public Library asked the people who participated why they were in the literacy classes and among the reasons they gave were:

> Fill out application forms and get better jobs, read the papers one signs, use a telephone directory, . . . read street signs, . . . read letters brought home from school by children, read bedtime stories to small children, read labels and directions on medicines, cosmetics, food packages, detergents, etc., . . . understand Social Security, Medicare, welfare . . . instructions. . . .[3]

I can find nothing in Hilton's ideal system that would help Cleveland's illiterates very much, and I rather suspect that financing Hilton's project would torpedo Cleveland's. That's our dilemma in thinking about the first step into ALA's second century. Unless we have a pretty solid idea of what kind of society we are providing with information we may end up running rapidly backwards.

Now I'm very reluctant to play seeress and look into crystal balls to describe the future. Not out of any false modesty, you understand, but because I believe the future is the future and that what we do or fail to do creates that future. But I have heard some errant nonsense about this post-industrial society we're evolving into.

Pooh-Bah-in-Chief of the futurologists is Daniel Bell whose *The Coming of Post-Industrial Society* (1973) signaled a new fad. Bell sees some immense societal changes as a result of advances in technology.

> By producing more goods at less cost, technology has been the chief engine of raising the living standards of the world. The achievement of technology, the late Joseph Schumpeter was fond of saying, was that it brought the price of silk stockings within the reach of every shopgirl, as well as of a queen. But technology has not only been the means of raising levels of living, it has been the chief mechanism of reducing inequality within Western society.[1]

Well, I just saw the Queen of England attend a gala in her honor at Covent Garden on TV. I work with a couple of dozen library clerks (the equivalent of Schumpeter's shopgirls), and I can assure you the clerks don't dress like the queen, don't eat like the queen, don't spend their days or their nights like the queen, certainly don't have her job security and, even if they can afford silk (silk?) are no more equal to the queen—or to her nontitled counterparts in this country—than they ever were.

In "areas of the world which have become highly industrialized," a recent paper tells me, "society is increasingly characterized by having its labor force concentrated in the sphere of services, professional and technical, rather than . . . extractive industries . . . or manufacturing and distributive industries." One result of this change will be that

> . . . our primary institutions are expected to be the university, the academic institute, the research corporation, the industrial laboratory, the library; our economic ground, science-based industries; our primary resource, human capital; our political problem, science policy and education policy; our structural problem, the balancing of the interests of the public and private sectors. Upward

access through the social-economic strata of this society is assumed to depend upon advanced education even more than at present.[7]

This analysis, based on a number of recent publications by assorted pundits, reminds me of the administration courses I took in library school. It was assumed that every one of the students was destined to become the director of the Library of Congress and that we were all panting to discover how to get more work out of all those lazy bums we were going to administer. Nobody even whispered naughty words like "money" or "unions," and even "job" was a no-no. We were all going to get "positions."

Well, it's true that our society has fewer farmers and miners and fewer assembly-line workers in the labor force than we used to have, but outside of that, the analysis sounds like still another fairy tale. It certainly doesn't describe the society I see about me. Our post-industrial society is a world of work and not very exciting or interesting work. Economist Robert Heilbroner warns against glib assumptions about our post-industrial society. He says:

> Let me warn against the misconception of . . . a massive emigration from industrial work. Nothing of that kind is visible. . . . The industrial "core" remains roughly constant . . . the industrial factory worker . . . continues to account for approximately the same proportion of the total work experience of the community . . . the blue collar group constituted 25.5 percent of the labor force in 1900 and 34.9 percent in 1968.[5]

Sure, we've got more service workers but they're not professionals and technicians for the most part. Service workers are janitors, bartenders, dishwashers, midwives, baggage porters, hairdressers, police and firefighters, more than nineteen million of them according to the 1970 census and more than twenty-three million in 1975. And in most of these jobs, upward access doesn't depend on advanced education. There isn't any upward access—and these days, more and more often, not even a job.

REPETITIVE, MINDLESS ROUTINE WORK

And we've got more clerical workers. It used to be that clerks were differentiated from blue collar workers by somewhat higher wages, somewhat higher prestige, and somewhat higher chances of making decisions within their jobs. No more. Rationalization, mechanization, technology and science have all been enlisted to reduce clerical work to the same kind of repetitive, mindless routines the factory worker has always known. What characterizes a large part of the labor force is, in the words of Harry Braverman,

> . . . the growth at one pole of an immense mass of *wage-workers*. The apparent trend to a large nonproletarian 'middle class' has resolved itself into the creation of a large proletariat in a new form. In its conditions of employment, this working population has lost all former superiorities over workers in industry, and in its scales of pay has sunk almost to the very bottom.[2]

The professionals—the engineers and doctors and librarians who constitute about 20% of the labor force—work, many of them, under no better conditions. More and more of them are employees in large enterprises, deciding very little about their jobs and performing routine and repetitive tasks.

So for whom is the university, the research corporation and the library the primary institution? Whose economic ground is science-based industry? Whose political problem is science policy and education policy? Only that small select minority in our society who make the decisions that determine how the rest of us live—and work, *if* we can find work. The institution that most governs our lives is not the university nor the library but the corporation.

THE CORPORATE POWER

John Kenneth Galbraith says:

> The institution that most changes our lives . . . is the modern corporation. Week by week, month by month, year by year, it exercises a greater influence on the way we live than unions, universities, politicians, the government.[4]

The economic ground most of us will be most deeply engaged in is sheer survival as we're buffeted between inflation, fear of losing our jobs and increasing taxes. And our political problem? Neither science policy nor education policy, except peripherally, but latching on to some political power, enough to pass legislation serving the majority.

Well, given that kind of society, what kinds of information do most people need? I don't know. That doesn't seem to be the question our profession has been addressing. The library schools seem to be involved in teaching young White males how to succeed older White males in the information world. The National Commission seems to be concerned with guaranteeing the establishment of a *profitable* information network. The information industry seems to be engaged in lobbying for the private sector's right to design and profit from an international automated information pipeline. The academic libraries seem to be engaged in serving rich faculty who can afford fees for services. The public libraries seem to be deeply concerned with the quickest way to slap user fees on their services. Maybe school libraries are still interested in finding out what information most kids need and giving it to them—but funding school libraries seems to be going out of style. So before we can even approach the subject of access, maybe we need to devote our collective minds to the problem of what kind of information most people need access to. What most people don't need most of the time is a bibliography. And to most librarians and information scientists, that *particular* nonneed translates itself into a generalized, "Well, then, they don't need information."

Let me give you two examples of a very simple thesis: all people need information, but the kinds of information most people need is different in form and content from that required and made available by the educated elite.

THE VITAL NEED FOR INFORMATION

During a recent international conference on the "Origins of Human Cancer" sponsored by the Cold Spring Harbor Laboratory, the Harvard School of Public Health, and the National Cancer Institute, it was reported that recent studies show a huge increase in the risk of breast cancer and cancer of the lining of the uterus for the millions of women who have been given estrogens during the menopause.[8] Other studies show an increase in breast and womb cancer among populations whose diet is heavy in animal fat, especially when livestock are fattened on synthetic estrogens, as they are in this country. Now the information that most women in this country need is the information that estrogens injected into their own bodies or those of the animals they'll consume are dangerous to their health, but our information networks are not designed to give us access to such information. Scientists have access to it and the pharmaceutical industry has access to it and agri-business has access to it; but they're not about to make it generally available and neither are the designs of the leaders in librarianship and information science.

If you walked into any library in the country today and asked a layperson's question: Will taking estrogens during menopause increase the risk of cancer? you would not get a straight "yes" no matter how sophisticated a database the librarians manipulated for you—at a fee.

My second example is a report of a survey carried out in Finland:

> In 1972, the workers on a building site near Helsinki, who were living in prefabricated huts on the site because their home towns were too far away, were interviewed as to their working conditions, the recreational opportunities available to them, hygienic conditions, etc. The interview situation was based on a questionnaire which had been filled out previously. In these interviews, 60 percent of the respondents stated that they were entirely satisfied with the conditions prevailing on the site. When, however, the questionnaire papers were put aside and the respondents were (deliberately) engaged by the interviewer in free conversation, the same individuals brought out numerous and serious complaints about conditions which obviously had bothered them considerably.[9]

Elina Suominen, the author of the article, is a researcher at the Finnish Ministry of Justice and secretary of that country's National Committee on Data Systems. In a most perceptive analysis she goes on to say:

> The media use primarily the language and the terminology familiar to the highly educated section of the population, the terminology which those with less education have not completely mastered. They talk about issues so abstract that they do not reach the audience, and in a manner shunned by the working class. Furthermore, messages with a 'serious' subject, such as history, politics, or economics, are carried out primarily by those media (newspapers, books, etc.) which

are favored by the educated classes, whereas television, weekly magazines, and the like tend to stress entertainment and sensational material. With the constant increase in the share of 'light communication' produced outside Finland, chiefly with American capital, the share of national material is declining. Anxieties, fears, and a shortened span of interest are becoming more and more common. Parents, struggling with money and housing difficulties, do not have either the ability or the time to guide their children in the best use of media. In other words, those who have the greatest objective need of information often feel the least subjective need. This conclusion has far-reaching consequences. A society based on material inequality is built in part precisely on this disproportion between objective and subjective information need. For example, when Elizabeth Taylor spent the night in a Helsinki hotel on her way to Leningrad, dozens of papers described her 300 pounds of luggage, her male companion, and her clothes. If a survey had been done at this point, it would have shown Finns to be considerably better informed about Miss Taylor's baggage than about the difficult and complex labor negotiations going on in the country at the same time. In objective terms, the contract concerning wage and price increases had a considerably more far-reaching effect on the everyday life of a vast majority of the population than the number of Miss Taylor's suitcases.[9]

DROP THE "PRIME MARKET" APPROACH

So the central problem in public access to information is what kinds of information we're giving the public access to. And the providers of information, *we librarians,* need to dedicate ourselves to the discovery of the information needs of *most* people, not of an elite already fairly well served, and to providing that information rapidly, intelligibly and responsibly. The reasons we have not done so are subtle and complex, and we need to struggle to understand them better. Most of us are not consciously the tools of rapacious agri-business, deliberately keeping information from people. Even agri-business isn't consciously doing that. But agri-business is out to increase its profits and will not disseminate information which endangers those profits. And librarians have lent themselves to that restrictive aspect of information gathering and dissemination. Out of a combination of timidity, irresponsibility, snobbery, ignorance and miseducation we have never spoken for the right of *everyone* to information.

As a matter of fact, some pretty high-level library leaders have gone on record urging us to stop worrying about the information needs of some lost souls. Our own Robert Wedgeworth suggests, "Young people who come from poor, broken homes, belong to street gangs, and are flunking out of school are not our prime market." What is it exactly we are "marketing?" To whom? I would suggest, in contradiction to Mr. Wedgeworth's analysis, that unless we find the ways to provide necessary information, as well as food and housing and clothing, to those same young people from poor, broken homes, they will people our prisons and hospitals and welfare centers, and that Mr. Wedgeworth's more lucrative "markets" will be devoting lots of energy to paying huge societal costs.

Even if we were to recognize, collect and disseminate the kind and the form of information a majority of our population needs, we have allowed so much of the business mentality to seep in that our ability to function as professional information-providers has already been deeply eroded. Not just by modeling library organization on business organization. That's bad enough because it often results in libraries which simply have not conceived that real needs aren't always best served by "efficient" organizations. Profits may be, but not necessarily user needs. What's worse is an indecent rush to make use of new technology without considering the most socially effective ways to pay for that technology. User fees are often the *only* approach ever considered, with no concern for possible alternatives and with no concern for the social inequities that user fees in a public service impose. I must sound a warning here that the indiscriminate imposition of fees for library services may be the library profession's contribution to the breakdown of public access to information. Public access must not be taken to mean the "rich public's" access.

WE, TOO, SHALL OVERCOME

We have been too timid to demand money and resources at least equal to those distributed to the private sector. We have been frightened of taking responsibility for the accuracy of the information we do dispense. We have secretly relished the "importance" of our calling, the provision of information to the "decision-makers," complacently accepting a hierarchy of information needs and users. We have been content to define intellectual freedom as an abstract concept and I hear ominous reverberations that taking action for educational programs against racism and sexism is somehow to be equated with censorship. And we have, even more ominously, refused to take a stand for the principle of free services, provided by our society as a whole to guarantee equality in access. Not that I believe librarians to be incapable of courage and responsibility and generosity and just plain good sense. On the contrary! I believe that most of us, most of the time, want so much to provide the widest kind of access to the most accurate kind of information that we shall collectively find ways to overcome tremendous pressures. But only when we understand that inequality in public access to information can determine whether our society continues to survive.

REFERENCES

1. Bell, Daniel. *The Coming of Post-Industrial Society.* New York: Basic Books, 1973. p. 188-9.
2. Braverman, Harry. *Labor and Monopoly Capital; the Degradation of Work in the Twentieth Century.* New York: Monthly Review Press, 1974. p. 355.

3. Brown, Eleanor Frances. *Library Service to the Disadvantaged.* Metuchen, NJ: Scarecrow Press, 1971. p. 450.
4. Galbraith, John Kenneth. "UGE: The Inside Story," *Horizon* 19(1):5 (March 1977).
5. Heilbroner, Robert. "Economic Problems of a 'Post-Industrial' Society," *Dissent* (Spring 1973). p. 163-76.
6. Hilton, Howard J. "An Ideal Information Access System: Some Economic Implications," in *Information for Action: From Knowledge to Wisdom.* Kochen, Manfred, ed. New York: Academic Press, 1975. p. 206-7.
7. Marquis, Rollin P. "Post-Industrial Society and the Growth of Information: The Impact on Libraries," *The Information Society: Issues and Answers.* E. J. Josey, ed. Phoenix, AZ: The Oryx Press, 1978.
8. Randal, Judith. "The Social Origins of Cancer," *Change* 8(10):54-5 (November 1976).
9. Suominen, Elina. "Who Needs Information and Why," *Journal of Communication* 26(4):116-8 (Autumn 1976).

Literature on Problems of Access in Libraries

by Miriam Braverman

The social, economic and technological changes in society converge when we are examining access, the final link between the library clientele and the libraries' resources. What is most interesting, when we examine the literature, is that, often, articles describing technological changes in some libraries become almost instantly obsolete, because the rate of response to technology in these libraries is so rapid. On the other hand, other libraries struggle with the most basic problems of survival, such as keeping the doors of the library open. It becomes clear, as we follow the issues, the problems and the trends in the literature, that to guarantee equal access to resources, the changes in the world around us require public policy revisions and decisions which, although heavily debated in the literature, are hardly being implemented with the same decisive speed as the application of technological innovation.

ON-LINE SERVICES

The most dramatic developments in recent years have been in library use of on-line services. Since 1974 the use of on-line databases, particularly bibliographic databases, has skyrocketed. In a survey of the development of on-line services since the 1960s, Jeffrey Gardner and David Wax describe the early forms of organization for delivery of on-line service, which moved in the 1970s to greater use of commercial firms, contributing to the rapid growth of this sector. While access to databases is facilitated through the use of a broker, the need for control of the quality of the service, and the trend to serving an elite group dictated by fee charges, have made this development a mixed blessing.[29]

The introduction of fee charges as the use of commercial information brokers expands has become a major issue of debate in the profession. There seem to be three schools of thought. One is represented by the spokesmen for the private sector, among whom is Paul Zurkowski, who believes that information controlled by the marketplace is most responsive to the user—whether the currency used to purchase information is money from those who have it, or vouchers backed by some government revenue source for those who don't.[76]

A second school of thought believes in cooperative types of arrangements between the public and private information sectors, a thesis described by Barbara Slanker, using as examples the Minneapolis Public Library, Chicago Public Library, and EDITEC, an Illinois-based commercial firm.[68]

Strong disagreement with both of these ideas is expressed by Fay Blake. Responding to Barbara Slanker's ideas, Ms. Blake and Jane Irby argue that the two sectors cannot be successful in a cooperative relationship because of the differences in goals and constituencies. As examples, they describe the experiences in four California libraries with Lockheed's DIALOG system and that of the Peninsula Library System Community Information Project.[3] The economics of user charges will result, say Ms. Blake and Edith Perlmutter, not in a more effective system for meeting user needs, as Zurkowski states, but in shrinking services to a small group who can pay.[4]

A most interesting phenomenon in the information broker field is the growth in the number of free-lance salesmen of information services. An estimated five to ten million dollar industry in 1974,[22] they give the kind of tailor-made service which libraries cannot or will not provide. Their relation to library institutions and their place in a national information network are important considerations to which an entire issue of the *Bulletin of the American Society for Information Science* is devoted.[36]

Who have been using the databases and what have their experiences been? Systematic studies by the profession itself have not yet appeared. Both System Development Corporation and Lockheed, two major suppliers of on-line services, have recently produced studies dealing with these questions. The SDC study reports on the experience of commercial and industrial organizations, colleges and universities and Federal government agencies, the categories with heaviest use of the services of ten major suppliers.[71] The Lockheed study reported on a two year experience with their own system in eight public libraries.[27] This experiment is being extended for another year, to assess the affect of charging patrons the full cost of on-line searching.

The proliferation of a variety of databases, many of which are combined in the service of one broker but must be searched separately, represents a chaotic situation demanding criteria for evaluation and selection. Martha Williams identifies these criteria[73] and in educating the profession to be critical in approaching database service, can help improve the quality of the service we provide the public.

A most interesting question, as we hurtle precipitously into the world of computer-based services, is how present on-line services are shaping the nature of information. M. Dillon sees the necessity for shifting the database information from basic to applied science, from documentation to problem solving.[21]

And what about information for human needs? An important survey of databases geared to this type of information need found only a handful computerized or geared for computerization. And while I & R center files are being developed by libraries and by social agencies around the country, many of the same problems relating to quality control in on-line services discussed by Martha Williams—subject coverage, consistency, need for standardization, access points for searching—apply to I & R files.[74]

THE BUDGET CRUNCH AND A NEW LOOK AT ORGANIZATION AND PRACTICES

While technology has opened up new dimensions in access to resources, severe constraints have been visited on many libraries, affecting access. Among these constraints have been rising costs, shrinking budgets and a declining school age population. Prodded by these constraints, many libraries have instituted cooperative acquisitions and resource sharing, transcending the old interlibrary loan concepts and procedures. Research libraries have been most active in this area. Research libraries need to do more than organize cooperation, however, says Richard De Gennaro;[19] they have to give up their hangups on size and numbers, improving their technical and organizational mechanisms for materials collection, with the large libraries "serving as resources for other libraries rather than models." Zeroing in on a particular thorny budget problem of libraries, the escalating cost of periodicals, concurrent with escalating production of serial titles, Mr. De Gennaro elaborates on suggested changes in periodical purchasing and weeding.[20]

The economic realities which have forced libraries into resource sharing have also raised questions about changes in institutional patterns to respond to new political and social realities—changes, as we have said, which are more in the debating stages than the implementation stages.

Some university librarians are concerned with the decline of the subject-divisional organization,[39] particularly its effectiveness as contrasted with a document delivery system.[23]

The need and effectiveness of the neighborhood branch library system, the keystone of public library service in the past, is being questioned, as branch library services in cities are eroded by the pressure of fiscal crisis.[8] Would the problems of providing services to city populations be alleviated by consolidating with systems beyond old political boundaries—county or multi-county areas? The proposal by Alex Ladenson for a Metropolitan Library Authority has elicited mixed reactions.[40] New York State public library systems have for some years transcended local political jurisdictional lines, but the free direct access policy created frictions, described and discussed in a report of the New York Commissioner of Education.[63] College librarians, too, have problems with serving users outside their jurisdictions.[44]

It is the schools, however, which have borne the brunt of citizen frustration with economic problems of rising taxes and inflation, and school librarians and libraries have been affected in a variety of ways. No adequate national survey exists which can tell us how service in school libraries has been affected in the past few years by teachers' strikes, failure of communities to pass school budgets, and school closings because of lack of funds. However, an interesting challenge to school libraries and their responsibility in information dissemination is laid down by D. Philip Baker, who believes that recent state court decisions mandating equality of access to education will eventually be judicially interpreted to mean equal access to information as well, decisions which will affect public as well as school libraries and force the two institutions to face giving children and young people access which has heretofore been spotty.[2]

Debates and discussions regarding guidelines for service and implementation stressing the community and the individual client, actual or potential, are taking place among many types of libraries. New approaches by public libraries,[5] reference librarians,[17] adult, young adult and childrens' librarians[1] have been developed. Substantive institutional change needed to meet new concepts of service has not appeared.

NETWORKING

There is one area where discussion and debate are combined with rapid and important developments, and this is in networking. It is obviously an idea whose time has come, and the National Commission on Libraries and Information Science has put the concept into the domain of public policy, and with it, the discussions and the developments take on an added urgency.

The proliferation of networks is closely tied to the increased use of on-line services. Early use of computers for technical services has expanded, as we have seen, to give people access to bibliographic data, and, in some cases, documentation. Technological capability makes it possible for people to browse through the computer in related classified areas,[11] extending access for the patron through a different type of network.

With all the discussion for a national network, encouraged by the NCLIS report,[34] the realities in networking today are still on a local, state and regional basis.[43]

Public library networks, with which we have had some years of experience, were surveyed and studied by Genevieve Casey, selecting for more detailed observations the systems in New York, California, Illinois, Maryland and Washington State, as well as SLICE as a representative of a multi-state network.[14] Among her conclusions were that people usually enter a network through the public library, and that college students, researchers and professionals are the heaviest users of the services, while children and high school students are usually excluded. These conclusions take on added importance when we consider that the findings concerning who uses the networked services coincides with that of who uses the on-line services.

What is the role and function of the reference librarian in a networked society? Do networks increase efficiency and decrease costs? Will the response to clients' requests be as effective when handled through a remote machine as when there is personal interaction between the reference librarian and the client? These are questions asked by Beverly Lynch, and still effectively unanswered.[48] The implications of these questions with relation to the concerns of the reference librarians when confronted with networks is very important, since, as was pointed out in the *Lockheed Two Year Interim Report,* the attitudes of the reference librarians are very important in the effectiveness of the implementation of on-line services.

There have been interesting mutations in cooperation among libraries which could be instructive and helpful for future planning. These include the Indiana Information Retrieval System,[49] the Minnesota Health Science Libraries,[52] the Library of Congress' regional networks for service to the blind and physically handicapped,[41] the study of the cooperative trends between public libraries and institutional libraries in Ohio,[47] and the Martin Luther King, Jr., Hospital Library, which meets the resource needs not only of the hospital staff but also of community health workers, dietitions, nurses in outreach programs, career guidance for high school and community college students, and patients.[34]

With the technological capability already at hand for any system of bibliographic control the library community might propose, the problem of what kind of system will meet whose needs is paramount. These and other problems were addressed by a seminar at the University of Chicago Graduate Library School, papers to be published by *Library Quarterly* in July 1977.

Meanwhile, are we addressing ourselves to the problems of social policy which will cope with the questions posed at the University of Chicago meeting? Are information networks common carriers, like public utilities?[57] What type of policy will insure that the information-poor will have equal access with the elite who currently benefit from networks and the new technology?

THE INFORMATION-RICH AND THE INFORMATION-POOR

Since the 1960s and the support to libraries from LSCA, ESEA and HEA funds, there has been an increasing sensitivity to information needs of various groups in the country's populations and efforts to refashion library programs to meet what the profession has perceived them to be. There has been a large body of literature on this, but it is still unclear whether the bulk of the literature is matched by increased effectiveness in programs to reach the social, class and ethnic groups who have traditionally been outside library service.

The information-poor have been defined and described by Thomas Childers and Joyce Post in terms of patterns of information-seeking behavior and areas of information need.[16] A compendium of articles identifying the specific groups among the information-poor, their characteristics and library needs as perceived by the writers, was one of the studies done for NCLIS.[46] General findings of a national survey of library services to the elderly in Indiana found only two percent of the aging in the United States receiving specific public library services, and identifies the constraints on this group.[26] Programs designed to deal with serious problems of literacy are described in two extremely useful publications.[65] An up-to-date report on library services to prisoners, a full issue of *Wilson Library Bulletin,* includes not only articles by librarians in a variety of institutions but, most important, includes one by the Inmate Library Committee at Soledad Prison.[9]

This article by the prisoners gets to the heart of the nagging question which, despite all the federal money and highly touted programs, remains with us—are we reaching the information-poor on their terms and with their input? Is what we need a "Foxfire" approach—a human and personalized approach transcending institutions and agencies?[24]

INFORMATION AND REFERRAL SYSTEMS

A relative newcomer in the arsenal of programs to reach the information-poor is Information and Referral. But it is not only the poor who are information-poor in our society when the concern is human need. The growth of bureaucracy concurrent with the fragmentation in the delivery of social services has made necessary information systems to guide people to needed services. Several sources of available federal funding have encouraged the development of I & R services, including Title XX of the Social Security Act, Title I of LSCA, and funding from Model Cities legislation and the National Science Foundation.

The idea of neighborhood branch libraries transformed into communications or information transfer centers, as the most cost-effective vehicle for delivery of I & R systems, is developed by Yin, Kenney and Possner in their study published by the Rand Corporation.[75] The beautiful logic of such a system is discussed by a social scientist as a result of a major study in social service delivery.[7] The major factors which make for an effective I & R system in public libraries are discussed in Thomas Childers' study of the five public libraries which developed pilot programs in this area.[15] Another I & R service, in the

Rochester and Monroe County (New York) Library System, is geared to serve primarily social agency people with their Human Services Directory available by subscription. The I & R specialist in that system also acts as a consultant for member libraries who wish to set up local I & R services.[6]

Libraries, however, must be aware of the systems developed under other auspices, how they work and who sponsors them. Some examples: San Diego (California) Information Center, with government information on local, state and federal levels;[13] the Dade County (Florida) Citizens Information and Service program sponsored by the United Fund and Metropolitan Dade County.[31] There are many others, and a subscription to the Newsletter of the Alliance of Information and Referral Services, 5020 North 20th St., Phoenix, Arizona 85016, keeps us updated on these programs.

There are many problems of skills and techniques in organization which are crucial to effective access in these services. Guides on sources and techniques in data gathering dependent on knowledge of community information needs are given in two publications, one related to urban needs and the other to rural population needs.[56] A video tape with a discussion by Major Owens on determining information needs, and filmed activities of the Yonkers (New York) Job Information Center and the Langston Hughes Library and Cultural Center, is unique.[45]

The organization of the services, the files, the training of the staff, are all crucial for effective access.[18]

THE RIGHT TO KNOW AND THE RIGHT TO BE LEFT ALONE

With the increasing awareness of the magnitude of the computerized "dossier society" and its threats to individual freedom and privacy, with the accompanying increase in public sentiment for the need for greater openness in government, vexing problems have developed in access to information. The right of a citizen to be left alone—based on the Fourth Amendment that "the right of the people to be secure . . . against unreasonable searches and seizures," and the right to know what the government does and what it collects from and about us—based on the First Amendment, have been enacted into legislation on federal and state levels in Freedom of Information Acts and the Privacy Act of 1974 (federal), which, when juxtaposed, create conflicts.

The dilemma is posed and dissected by Lauri Provencher.[59] Allan Reitman, a civil liberties lawyer, gives guidelines on determining what he considers the primacy of one right over another.[61] A wide ranging discussion on a variety of facets of the problem, including the inadequacy of privacy safeguards as well as suggestions as to how to get information from the government, make up the bulk of an issue of the *Bulletin of the American Society for Information Science*.[28]

The Right to Know

The Freedom of Information Act is reprinted in full and then translated, section by section, into layman's language in a publication of the Church of Scientology.[33] This does not include the recent amendment. Having the right to the information is spurious, of course, without access to it, and this is the tough part. Local information is still the most difficult to come by and the need to develop a policy for dissemination is crucial. A model of such a policy is written up in the *Public Administration Review*.[70] The poor bibliographic access to government documents is one frustrating factor.[25] Another is that only half of the government information to which the public is entitled is announced publicly, while, for the rest, agencies use various mechanisms and routes to circumvent the law.[69]

One of the most useful studies helping us to understand the factors which encourage agencies to give out information, and also the strategies used by others to circumvent information requests, was done by students at the Northwestern University School of Law. Field experiments were done with agencies in Chicago, Cook County and Illinois, but since bureaucracy is a universal phenomenon, the results of these studies are useful for us all.[60]

It is an archivist, James B. Rhoades, to whom we are indebted for articulating the need for greater public commitment on the part of our profession for opening up the heretofore closed information sources, with an emphasis on making state and local documents available to the public, particularly children in schools.[64]

The Right to be Left Alone

The provisions of the federal Privacy Act of 1974 are explained in the *Civil Service Journal.*[58]

A recent document which, although it is a product of the Ford administration, is of primary importance to us in the area of privacy since it represents the views of powerful centers in government, is the *National Information Policy, Report to the President of the United States.*[55] This document presents an overall program legislating boundaries between the Freedom of Information Act, the Privacy Act and the Federal Records Act. But it does not stop there, it recommends public policy in a host of related areas: extension of use of the Freedom of Information Act from corporations, the present chief users, to the general public; the private information sector and pricing policies, copyright and networks as public utilities; balancing competition and monopoly "in shaping the national information infra-structure," an issue of critical importance as the American Telegraph and Telephone Co. tries to push its bill through Congress to gain a monopoly over information transfer by legislating the use of telephone lines as the carrier. Libraries are mentioned once in relation to the publishing industry as two print-oriented groups that might fit in somewhere. If, as this document suggests, an Office of Information Policy is set up in the Executive Branch, the membership of this regulatory agency and its regulations and priorities will be critical not just for libraries, but for access to information by the citizens of this country. We need vigilance.

Librarians too have a need to understand the application of the laws in relation to their own records; we need to define our role in relation to confidentiality of records, not only borrowers' records, but those of library employees too. By supporting an overall national information policy, without exploring alternatives, we may be unleashing a "dybbuk."[32]

CENSORSHIP/INTELLECTUAL FREEDOM

It is no longer possible to sustain an unquestioned purist stance on the First Amendment, to be what Charles Rembar, the noted civil liberties attorney, called a "First Amendment Junkie."

Many individuals and groups have been examining the meaning and the application of the First Amendment, as it was interpreted in the past, and what its meaning is for the present.

One group which has been viewing with alarm the "new morality" or "amorality" which has extended the boundaries of the permissible in expression, whether reading, viewing or listening, have followed the lead of the President's Commission on Obscenity and Pornography to limit access to "pornography" to "young people"—age undefined.

The definition of pornography has eluded even Supreme Court justices, but a brave try, resulting in a useful and succinct resume was made by F. L. Marcuse. In his article he identifies factors which have been involved in the various and conflicting criteria defining pornography.[50]

The application of the doctrine of "community standards" which the Supreme Court ruled could define acceptable parameters of expression, was an issue in the Kanawha County, West Virginia textbook struggle. Despite the definitive professional statement in that fight,[37] there are still serious unresolved questions for many people:

> What are the legitimate powers of the state in educating children of social and religious minorities? At what point does the protection of minority rights become a minority tyranny? How far does parental authority extend in controlling children's reading? Can an electoral majority exile Darwin from the classroom library?[35]

Charles Rembar won prominence in the civil liberties struggle as the attorney for Grove Press in the suite that broke literary censorship in winning the right to publish *Tropic of Cancer* and *Lady Chatterley's Lover*. That, he now says, was the old "obscenity" fight, and it is over. The printed word cannot be suppressed, because reading is a voluntary activity. However, he feels, with film and TV new problems arise. Children who are exploited by pornographic film makers by involving them in sexual activity need protection. Children also need protection from abuse which comes out of the TV set. Rembar defines other limits which, because through the media they involve action mixed with expression, he does not consider violations of First Amendment rights.[62]

There is a sharp dispute in our profession over the meaning of racism and sexism awareness in relation to the Library Bill of Rights. The resolution of Council, Summer 1976, recommending efforts in the profession to raise the consciousness of librarians in identifying racism/sexism, and racist/sexist materials and the First Amendment are considered by some a violation of the Library Bill of Rights, while others see it as an extension of First Amendment rights. We can look forward to a flood of literature on the subject. For purposes of this paper, we shall single out three articles which bear on the subject: an historical analysis by Evelyn Geller of the early role of librarians as "arbiters of morality through control over reading matter," with the principle of intellectual freedom not adopted until 1939;[30] an article by Dorothy Broderick on intellectual freedom as having been defined by librarians in accordance with the dominant value system of society, including racist materials in collections which violate the intellectual freedom of those victimized by these materials;[10] Norma Fox Mazer's position that racism in books is enraging and painful for all readers, but the children can "sort out things for themselves" and, in the trade-off, censorship is a greater risk.[51]

The responsibility of librarians working with young people in disseminating materials containing ever-escalating levels of violence and brutality is another facet of our debate on First Amendment rights.[12]

While we debate these important issues, there are still censors working to deny young people, in schools and public libraries, access to materials whose value is recognized by a consensus in the profession and in the literary world. The fight in Rochester, Michigan, to retain Vonnegut's *Slaughterhouse Five* in the school library,[38] and the decision of the Oklahoma County Libraries System, after a long, hard struggle, to maintain open access to all materials for all patrons, are useful prototypes, as well as needed encouragement in maintaining rights of young people, so often violated.[53] Violations of people's First Amendment rights do not always come from crusading groups or rampaging authorities. Violation, as Judith Serebnick found out in a recent survey, can come from librarians practicing self-censorship.[67]

CENSORSHIP

The new copyright law will go into effect January 1, 1978. A special issue of the *ALA Washington Newsletter,* now available through ALA, gives brief highlights of the law, its provisions which are important to libraries, and the government documents essential for understanding the law.

ALA's Washington office urges librarians to become familiar with the law and to begin its implementation, for the fair use doctrine is codified in it, as well as the limits and the permissible areas for dissemination of materials through libraries.[72]

It is interesting that the law provides for an American Television and Radio Archive. A few years ago Vanderbilt University and the Columbia Broadcasting System were doing legal battle over the right claimed by the Vanderbilt TV News Archives to make available the evening newscasts of the major networks.[42] The case was settled, but the issue remains: what is fair use in nonprint media?

Obviously, we are at the beginning of a long process of definition, as well as enforcement and implementation. But as we proceed to try to live in the new world of copyright, we might keep in mind the words of Barbara Ringer:

> If authors lose individual control over their own works, *1984* may be here, and sometime in the 1980s perhaps, the combination of tyranny and technocracy could combine to destroy not only freedom of expression and the quality of life, but human culture itself.[66]

Ms. Ringer's appeal is appropriate as well to the spread in our profession of unbridled technology, expressed by some of the writers we discussed. Without social policy formulated to provide free and equal access to library materials as a social good, Ms. Ringer's bleak prognosis may become reality.

REFERENCES

1. ALA Task Force. "Guidelines for Work with Adults, Young Adults and Children," *Library Journal* 98:2606-9 (September 1973).
2. Baker, D. Philip. "School and Public Library Programs and Information Dissemination," *SMQ* 5:119-27 (Winter, 1976).
3. Blake, Fay M. and Jane Irby. "The Selling of the Public Library," *Drexel Library Quarterly* 12:149-59 (January/April 1976).
4. Blake, Fay M. and Edith L. Perlmutter. "Libraries in the Marketplace: Information Emporium of People's University?" *LJ* 99:108-11 (January 15, 1974).
5. Bloss, Meredith. "Standard for Public Library Service—Quo Vadis?" *LJ* 101:1259-63 (June 1, 1976).
6. Bovay, Sue. "Community Information Service in the Monroe County Library System: A Model," *Drexel Library Quarterly* 12:93-110 (January/April 1976).
7. Boyle, John M. "Urban Information Systems: A Social Science Perspective on Their Design and Implementation," *Drexel Library Quarterly* 12:27-48 (January/April 1976).

8. "The Branch Library in the City: Options for the Future—A Mini Symposium," *LJ* 102:161-73 (January 15, 1977).
9. "Breaking In: Library Service to Prisoners," *Wilson Library Bulletin* 51: (February 1977).
10. Broderick, Dorothy. "Censorship Reevaluated," *LJ* 96:3816-8 (November 15, 1971).
11. Butler, Brett. "State of the Nation in Networking," *Journal of Library Automation* 8:200-20 (September 1975).
12. Campbell, Patty. "Se Habla YA Aqui," *Booklegger* 3:48-9 (Autumn 1976); Braverman, Miriam. "Songmy: Human Imperative," *School Library Journal* 16:27-9 (January 1970).
13. Canyon, Jim. "One-Stop Information Shopping: San Diego [California] Information Center handles all inquiries no matter which governmental level has ultimate responsibility," *Nation's Cities* 10:16-7 (December 1972).
14. Casey, Genevieve M. *The Public Library in the Network Mode: A Preliminary Investigation.* Washington, DC: U.S. Office of Education, May 1974. [Available through ERIC]
15. Childers, Thomas. "The Neighborhood Information Center Project," *Library Quarterly* 46:271-89 (July 1976).
16. Childers, Thomas and Joyce A. Post. *The Information-Poor in America.* Metuchen, NJ: Scarecrow Press, 1975.
17. "A Commitment to Information Services: Development Guidelines," *RQ* 15:327-30 (Summer 1976); Vavrek, Bernard. "Bless You Samuel Green: A Discussion of RASD's New Information Service Guidelines," *LJ* 101:971-3 (April 15, 1976); Rugh, Archie G. "Reference Standards and Reference Work: A Critique of the New RASD Guidelines 'A Commitment to Information Services'," *LJ* 101:1497-500 (July 1976).
18. Croneberger, Robert B., Jr. "Systems Organization and Data Collection;" Luck, Carolyn. "Staff Trainings for the Information Center," *Drexel Library Quarterly* 12:69-92 (January/April 1976); Hughes, Nola. "Providing I & R Services in Rural Areas," *Proceedings of the I & R Round Table at the 102nd Annual Forum, National Conference on Social Welfare* Phoenix, AZ: Alliance of Information and Referral Services, Inc., 1975. pp. 46-55; Gilbert, Frances. "Linking Community Consumers and Services—Classification or Chaos;" Deahl, Thomas. "Vocabulary Control in an Automated I & R Directory System;" Brooks, Rae and Dan Eastman. "Different Strokes: Response to Frances Gilbert," *Proceedings of the I & R Round Table,* 1975.
19. De Gennaro, Richard. "Austerity, Technology and Resource Sharing: Research Libraries Face the Future," *LJ* 100:917-23 (May 15, 1975).

20. De Gennaro, Richard. "Escalating Journal Prices: Time to Fight Back," *American Libraries* 8:69-74 (February 1977).

21. Dillon, M. "Impact of Automation on the Content of Libraries and Information Centers," *College and Research Libraries* 34:418-25 (November 1973).

22. Dodd, James B. "Information Brokers," *Special Libraries* 67:243-50 (May/June 1976).

23. Dougherty, R. M. and L. L. Bloomquist. *Improving Access to Library Resources: The Influence of Organization of Library Collections, and of User Attitudes Toward Innovated Services.* Metuchen, NJ: Scarecrow Press, 1974.

24. Ewart, Geraldine Sydney. "Endeavoring to Reach the Information-Poor," *Drexel Library Quarterly* 12:171-6 (January/April 1976).

25. Fass, E. M. "Government Information Services: or, Of Needles and Haystacks," *Drexel Library Quarterly* 10:123-46 (January/April 1974).

26. Feiste, K. L. "Indiana Libraries and Services to the Elderly: as reported in National Survey of Library Services to the Aging," *Focus* 28:14-9 (Winter 1974).

27. Firschein, Oscar and R. K. Summit. *Two Year Interim Report: Investigation of Public Library as a Linking Agent to Major Scientific, Educational, Social and Environmental Data Bases.* Palo Alto, CA: Lockheed Development Corp., 1976.

28. "Freedom of Information vs. Privacy: An Information Dilemma," a series of articles, *Bulletin of the American Society for Information Science* 3 (October 1976); Belair, Robert R. "Inadequate Privacy Protection in FOIA and the Privacy Act;" Lowe, Thomas C. "Computer Security Safeguards for Privacy: The Technical Role of NBS," [National Bureau of Standards]; Fisher, Paul L. "The Freedom of Information Center;" Neier, Aryeh. "The Freedom of Information Act, the Privacy Act—and You."

29. Gardner, Jeffrey J. and David M. Wax. "On-line Bibliographic Services," *LJ* 101:1827-33 (September 15, 1976).

30. Geller, Evelyn. "Intellectual Freedom: Eternal Principle or Unanticipated Consequence?" *LJ* 99:1364-7 (May 15, 1974).

31. Gonzalez, M. Q. "Community Information Center Project," *RQ* 12:360-1 (Summer 1973).

32. Harter, Stephen and Charles Busha. "Libraries and Privacy Legislation," *LJ* 101:474-81 (February 1, 1976); Crooks, Joyce. "Civil Liberties, Libraries and Computers," *LJ* 101:482-7 (February 1, 1976).

33. *How to Use the Freedom of Information Act.* Hollywood, CA: Council of Scientology Ministers, 1976.

34. Humphrey, M. Moss. "Martin Luther King, Jr. General Hospital and Community Involvement," *Bulletin of the Medical Library Assn.* 61:324-7 (July 1973).
35. Humphreys, James. "Textbook War in West Virginia," *Dissent* 23:164-70 (Spring 1976).
36. "Information Brokers: Can They Succeed?"; Goldstein, Seth. "Information on Demand: A Brief Summary;" "Information Brokers: Who, What, Why, How," *Bulletin of the American Society for Information Science* 2:10-20 (February 1976).
37. *Inquiry Report. Kanawha County, West Virginia: A Textbook Study in Cultural Conflict.* Washington, DC: National Education Association, February 1975.
38. "Intellectual Freedom and School Libraries: An In-Depth Case Study," *SMQ* 1:111-35 (Winter 1973).
39. Johnson, Edward R. "Subject-Divisional Organization in American University Libraries," *Library Quarterly* 47:23-42 (January 1977).
40. "The Jurisdictional Debate," *LJ* 99:2561 (October 15, 1974); Ladenson, Alex. "The Metropolitan Library Authority: A New Structure for Service," *LJ* 99:2935-8 (November 15, 1974); "Networks and Cooperation: The Jurisdictional Debate," *LJ* 99:3173-80 (December 15, 1974).
41. Kamisar, Hylda and Dorothy Pallet. "Talking Books and the Local Library," *LJ* 99:2123-5 (September 15, 1974).
42. Kies, Cosette. "Copyright vs. Free Access: CBS and Vanderbilt University Square Off," *Wilson Library Bulletin* 50:242-6, 1975.
43. Kittel, Dorothy A. *Trends in State Cooperation.* Washington, DC: U.S. Government Printing Office (-17-080-014670), 1977.
44. Laser, David. "Library Access and the Mobility of Users," *College and Research Libraries* 35:280-4 (July 1974).
45. *Libraries in the Streets.* Video tape (1/2", b&w). McLean, Polly. New York: Columbia University School of Library Service, 1974.
46. *Library and Information Service Needs of the Nation.* Proceedings of a Conference on the Needs of Occupational, Ethnic and Other Groups in the U.S. Washington, DC: GPO (5203-0033), 1974 (National Commission on Libraries and Information Science).
47. Lucioli, Clara E. *Trend Toward Partnership: A Study of State Institution and Public Library Cooperation in Ohio.* Columbus, OH: State Library of Ohio, 1976.
48. Lynch, Beverly P. "Networks and Other Cooperative Enterprises: Their Effect on the Function of Reference," *RQ* 15:197-202 (Spring 1976).

49. Marcus, M.J. "INDIRS: A New Public Resource," *Library Occurent* 24:235-40 (May 1973).
50. Marcuse, F.L. "Some Reflections on Pornography and Censorship," *Canadian Forum* 54:13-6 (March 1975).
51. Mazer, Norma Fox. "Comics, Cokes and Censorship," *Top of the News* 32:167-70 (January 1976).
52. McKloskey, Judith. "Minnesota's Health Science Libraries: Mission-Oriented Network," *Minnesota Libraries* 25:75-81 (Autumn 1976).
53. Meyers, Duane H. "Boys and Girls and Sex and Libraries: The Chronicle of One Library's Fight for Intellectual Freedom," *LJ* 102:457-63 (February 15, 1977).
54. National Commission on Libraries and Information Science. *Toward a National Program for Library and Information Services: Goals for Action.* Washington, DC: U.S. Government Printing Office, 1975.
55. *National Information Policy.* Report to the President of the United States, Submitted by the Staff of the Domestic Council Commission on the Right of Privacy, Hon. Nelson A. Rockefeller, Chairman. Washington, DC: National Commission on Libraries and Information Science, 1976.
56. Owens, Major R. and Braverman, Miriam. *Knowing Your Community: A Manual for Investigating and Identifying Information Needs in Neighborhoods.* New York: Columbia University School of Library Service, 1975; Gotsick, Priscilla. *Assessing Community Information and Service Needs.* Morehead, KY: Appalachian Adult Education Center, Rev. 1974. Now distributed by the American Library Association.
57. Parker, Edwin B. "Networks for an Information Society," *Bulletin of American Society for Information Science* 2:12-24 (June 1975).
58. "The Privacy Act," *Civil Service Journal* 16:1-6 (July/September 1975).
59. Provencher, Lauri. "Two Constitutional Rights Equal One Political Dilemma," *Center Magazine* 9:7-14 (January 1976).
60. "Public Access to Information: Research Study," *Northwestern University Law Review* 68:176-462 (May/June 1973).
61. Reitman, Alan. "Freedom of Information and Privacy: the Civil Libertarian's Dilemma," *American Archivist* 38:501-8 (October 1975).
62. Rembar, Charles. "Obscenity—Forget It," *Atlantic* 239:37-41 (May 1977).
63. *Report of the Commissioner of Education's Committee on Direct Access.* Albany, NY: University of the State of New York, State Education Department, 1974.

64. Rhoades, James B. "One Man's Hope for His Society, His Profession and His Country," *American Archivist* 39:5-13 (January 1976).
65. *The Right to Read and the Nation's Libraries.* Edited by the Right to Read Committee of the American Association of School Librarians, et al. Chicago: American Library Association, 1974; Lyman, Helen Y. *Literacy and the Nation's Libraries.* Chicago: American Library Association, 1977.
66. Ringer, Barbara. "Copyright and the Future of Authorship," *LJ* 101:229-32 (January 1, 1976).
67. Serebnick, Judith. "The 1973 Court Rulings on Obscenity: Have They Made a Difference?" *Wilson Library Bulletin* 50:304-10 (December 1975).
68. Slanker, Barbara Q. "Public Libraries and the Information Industry," *Drexel Library Quarterly* 12:139-49 (January/April 1976).
69. Smith, Ruth S. "Government Information Network—A Challenge of Size," *Bulletin of the American Society for Information Science* 2:19-21 (September 1975).
70. Stallings, C. Wayne. "Local Information Policy: Confidentiality and Public Access," *Public Administration Review* 34:197-204 (May/June 1974).
71. Wanger, Judith, Carlos and Mary Fishburn Cuadra. *Impact of Online Retrieval Services: A Survey of Users. 1974-1975.* Santa Monica, CA: System Development Corp., 1976.
72. *Washington Newsletter. Special Issue of ALA Washington Newsletter on New Copyright Law* 28 (November 15, 1976). (Reprints available from ALA, $2.00.)
73. Williams, Martha E. "Criteria for Evaluation and Selection of Data Bases and Data Base Services," *Special Libraries* 66:561-9 (December 1975).
74. Williams, Martha E. and Elaine Tisch Dunatov. "Data Bases for Coping with Human Needs," *Drexel Library Quarterly* 12:110-39 (January/April 1976).
75. Yin, Robert K., Brigitte L. Kenney, and Karen B. Possner. *Neighborhood Communications Centers: Planning I & R Services in the Urban Library.* Santa Monica, CA: Rand Corp. (R-1564-MP), November 1974.
76. Zurkowski, Paul. "Information Control and Marketplace Feasibility" in *Information Systems and Networks.* Sherrod, John, ed. Westport, CT: Greenwood Press, 1975.

Epilogue:
Issues and Answers:
The Participants' Views

by Joseph A. Boissé and Carla J. Stoffle

INTRODUCTION

The individuals brought together for the President's Program represented every conceivable aspect of library activity. Interest in, and concern for, libraries was the common denominator of the approximately 1,500 participants.

In order to provide the authors with the data necessary for this summarization, each table identified one of its members as the "recorder." These individuals were asked to jot down interesting ideas that surfaced during the discussion period which followed each of the formal presentations. The "recorders" were not expected to write essays; it was suggested that they confine their notes to brief comments, provocative questions and interesting ideas.

Following the annual ALA conference, the remarks were typed on individual 3 x 5 cards. The authors read through several thousand cards and attempted to group them around some recurring themes within each of the five general categories.

The following summary is a distillation, therefore, of the ideas which were recorded during the discussion portion of the President's Program. Great care has been taken by the authors to be as objective as possible and to merely present the ideas expressed by the conferees as they were recorded in Detroit.

Almost to an individual, the participants expressed not only a sense of satisfaction with the program but an appreciation for the opportunity presented by the program. While the annual conference has always provided persons interested in libraries with the opportunity to get together informally for an exchange of ideas, the Issues and Answers Program provided a more structured, planned methodology for generating such an exchange. One participant expressed it this way: It provided a mechanism for bringing together people from the trenches to grapple with issues and factors by which they are often manipulated but of which they are rarely the manipulators. The reluctance to deal with questions expressed by some of those present apparently did not hinder discussions which ranged far and wide.

Throughout the day, the theme which recurred with the most frequency was that of a need for more planning in the library world. Most people felt that libraries engage primarily in crisis service. There is no anticipation of problems on the horizon nor, obviously, of strategies to deal with them. It was the impression of participants that librarians and their administrators tend to view each crisis as an isolated problem. Libraries, they felt, have traditionally been, and continue to be, reactive rather than proactive in the matter of deciding their future.

THE IMPACT OF TECHNOLOGICAL CHANGE ON LIBRARIES

That the impact of technology on libraries and librarians is a concern of members of the association was underscored by the wealth of comments generated by Frederick Kilgour's talk. One of the themes extensively discussed was the humanizing/dehumanizing effect of technology. Comments ranged from the very negative to the emphatically positive with, as one would expect, the majority of participants espousing a position somewhere between the two. These moderate position persons believe that technology, in and of itself, is neither good nor bad. If it is used to enhance the service capability of an institution and to free up individuals so that they may provide a more individualized, personalized service, then technology can obviously be viewed as an advantage. On the other hand, if it becomes the master rather than the servant of libraries, it can hardly be considered a positive force. Several individuals suggested, to varying degrees of intensity, that Kilgour was too optimistic in his remarks.

The pessimism expressed by so many conferees appeared to be related to a strong criticism leveled at library administrators for inadequate planning with respect to technological applications in their institutions. A great number of comments stated that administrators appear to rush headlong into technological applications with little analysis or evaluation of its impact on the quality of service. Some individuals perceived a piecemeal approach to computerization rather than a well thought-out, planned, comprehensive, structured approach.

Perhaps the strongest comments relating to the question of technology were those which referred to its impact on personnel. Administrators were again taken to task for blithely assuming that personnel problems created by increased technological applications in libraries will be resolved simply by transfer within the institution or by attrition. What was alluded to by many and clearly expressed by a few was the belief that individual librarians are not as interchangeable within libraries as most administrators would like to assume.

Another group of comments would best be characterized as dealing with "fear." Librarians do not truly understand technology and, therefore, its perceived effects are threatening. Librarians feel threatened most by the employment insecurity they have observed in institutions which have computerized some operations. The changes brought about by technological applications further undermines an already shaky self-concept with respect to their professional role in society.

Given the far-ranging effects of technology both depicted by Kilgour and observed firsthand by many participants, it is not surprising that library education was the subject of much discussion. Here again, the diversity of comments only served to emphasize the catholicity of the participants in the program. The comment—voiced almost exclusively in the very recent past—that the library schools are turning out too many graduates surfaced repeatedly. A redirection of the curriculum was urged for library education with ALA identified as the catalyst responsible for bringing it about. Continuing education was seen as one answer for dealing with the problem of personnel displacement caused by technology.

The following represent just a few of the comments and suggestions made during the discussion:

- Can something (technology) which causes the elimination of positions really be a humanizing factor?
- We (at the conference) spent too much time discussing computers; we must look beyond that at other technological change.
- What was not discussed by Mr. Kilgour was the authoritarianism inherent in technological advances.
- Libraries should be examining their goals and realigning their priorities.
- Do costs associated with technology cause some services to be sacrificed in order to raise money to implement technological advances?
- If we don't examine the library's role in society ourselves, someone else will shape the future of our institutions.
- The fear of the new blots out any creativity that librarians may have.
- One result of unionization in libraries can be the slowing down of the change process.
- In library schools, there is too much training being done for old roles.
- Should we be training more people in a time of diminishing opportunities?
- Continuing education can help staff cope with the unsettling aspects of change.

THE IMPACT OF SOCIAL CHANGES ON LIBRARIES

More active involvement of librarians in the political process and the librarian's role as an agent for bringing about social change: these two issues have perhaps generated, in the library profession, more controversy during the past decade than any other issues. The annual ALA conferences of the late '60s and early '70s illustrated the intensity to which feelings rose on these issues. It was a time, in fact, when many feared that the Association itself would not, indeed, could not, survive. It could; it has; and the issues remain both important and controversial.

In the paper which he delivered to the program participants, New York State Senator Major Owens emphasized these very same issues. The intensity of the discussants' responses attests to the continued interest in the issues as well as to the ongoing disagreement related to them in the library world.

While a majority of the comments recorded during the discussion period supported a more activist role for librarians in both areas, those questioning or attacking that position represented a significant minority. In either case, arguments ranged from the philosophical to the very pragmatic. A number of participants expressed their concern in terms of budget: they fear to attract too much attention lest they displease those who approve library budgets in the community. On the whole, the comments generated on both of these topics were essentially the same as those which we have been hearing for the past decade:

- Timidity is our biggest enemy.
- Who should determine what social issues are to be supported by libraries/librarians?
- Librarians, on the whole, have a basic fear of confrontation and will do anything to avoid it.
- We must stress the redirection of library education so that it will address these issues and prepare librarians to deal with them.
- Should libraries put their budgets on the line by taking stands on public issues?
- Librarians have never responded to social change.
- We (librarians) have traditionally been elitists and have never reached out to the masses.
- Do we have a right to foist our ideas on the public?
- Libraries should provide equal access, but not get involved in social programs or support controversial activities.

On one point, there was virtual unanimous agreement: the visibility level of libraries must be raised in the community. The par-

ticipants were not in agreement, however, on just how that could be achieved. Their disagreement went back to the previous question: how active should they be in the political process and what role should they play in the dynamics of social change? Some people opted for a more traditional approach—work closely with the political elite who are currently in power. Others recommended a more direct approach:
- Create your own power base.
- Work with consumer groups and mobilize community support.
- Don't take budget cuts meekly, fight back, publicize the cuts and their effects on service.
- Don't shun the word "power." It can be just as positive as it can be negative.

In any case, the controversy is alive and the association remains divided on these issues. There was an implied undercurrent that uncertainty about our role as professionals was, at least in part, at the root of the problem. One of the participants opined that social upheavals have commonly been seen by the library world as generating a need to protect the profession itself rather than as an opportunity to meet the profession's responsibility to the public.

THE EFFECTS OF ECONOMIC CHANGE ON LIBRARIES

Thomas R. Buckman presented a very somber picture of the impact which economic conditions might have on libraries in the future. He attempted to depict realistically and forcefully the pressures which will come at libraries from all directions as available resources decrease and costs increase. The audience generally perceived his remarks to be pessimistic and, where they felt that Kilgour was too optimistic earlier in the day, Buckman was faulted for what some called his "doomsday" approach.

Several people stated that they did not understand economics adequately to be able to deal with this segment of the program. Many wondered whether the administrators who ran the nation's libraries adequately understood these forces to be able to deal with them. Related to this thought was another: libraries are simply buffeted by the economic forces surrounding them and have no role in controlling these forces. The feelings of uncertainty and insecurity voiced by a number of individuals in earlier discussion periods surfaced again.

As a result of Dr. Buckman's remarks, a number of people commented on the question of service for a fee or information for a fee. The question was a major topic of the fifth segment of the program and will be dealt with later in this summary.

That Buckman's paper was, from the point of view of those present, the most difficult to understand, seems to be borne out by the paucity of comments it generated in comparison with the other segments of the program. However, some of the most interesting and imaginative comments emerged during this discussion period:

- Tight economic times may allow the imaginative director to make adjustments which would be extremely unpopular at other times.
- Perhaps libraries should declare bankruptcy and go on to a reorganization and complete rethinking of their role in society.
- One outcome of Dr. Buckman's talk was that I now view information strictly as a commodity with a price tag.
- These problems stress once again the need for librarians to stretch their minds, to break out of familiar patterns, to think beyond the familiar horizons within which they feel so comfortable.
- Perhaps we should abandon the term "free public library," because it is a misnomer since nothing is free. We should use a term such as "public information center," which will stress the "public good" aspect of the library.
- To survive, libraries need to become more visible; therefore, why not have floating information librarians stationed in airports, supermarkets and department stores (to name a few) with telephone access to information materials.
- This paper helped me realize how much of a stake librarians have in the future economics of the information business.

With respect to this segment of the program, probably the most obvious conclusion is that library schools and the Association should develop methods for helping librarians better understand the economic factors with which libraries must deal if they are to survive.

THE NEW ROLE OF LIBRARIANS AS PROFESSIONALS

Undoubtedly the most basic issue dealt with by the President's Program is the identity crisis of professional librarians. It is not a new problem but it has been exacerbated by the rapid changes taking place in libraries and in society in general. How problems resulting from growing technologies, worsening economic conditions, declining literacy levels, increasing attacks from would-be censors, rising unionization of public employees, etc. are dealt with by libraries will be determined in large part by how librarians see their roles. This role definition will, in turn, influence how society perceives, supports and uses its libraries in the next decade.

How do librarians perceive their roles? Are the roles actually changing? Although no complete definition of role emerged, the conferees offered several possibilities. The most frequently mentioned was that librarians are information transfer agents and as such, their roles have not changed over time; only the tools and methods for accomplishing them have changed. In fact, one participant offered that the "New role of [the] librarian is the old role which has never been achieved." Other participants saw the librarians as teachers, leaders, public relations specialists, interpreters of needs, systems linkers, advocates of social change, information producers and packagers, and protectors of society's right to information. Implicit in all comments was the concern for service and meaningful human interaction. The participants generally saw librarians as active rather than passive agents in society.

The one glaring gap in the discussion of professional roles during this session was the lack of attention to the librarian as a collector and organizer of materials. It appeared that most of the conferees either had no idea of what professionals would be doing in technical services given the range of technological applications in that area, or they felt librarians would be generally phased out in technical services in the future. Perhaps the answer lies somewhere between the two. It does appear, however, that there is a definite need for further information concerning the impact of technology on the professional librarian in technical services.

Along with the discussion of the professional roles themselves, many comments were directed to many of the needs and concerns of professional librarians. Continuing education, better library school education, more action from the American Library Association, and greater communication and cooperation between librarians in differing types of libraries were all touched on. Representative statements are listed below.

Continuing Education

- Librarians should be required to go back to school, take seminars, or go to workshops at least once a year.
- Administrators should push their staff harder to be involved in continuing education programs and should provide time off with financial support to help those that do.
- Continuing education plays an important part in helping librarians meet the demands of increased service, involvement, and flexibility. There is a need to increase opportunities for working librarians to avail themselves of continuing education programs via in-house training at the local, state and national levels.
- Librarians need time to be able to take courses, attend conferences to increase their professional knowledge and help their patrons.
- Librarians should have allotted time to study, attend workshops, etc. to increase their knowledge.
- Continuing education for librarians is important and programs should be developed more fully.
- In-service training of staff in the use of computers is essential.

Library Schools

- Library schools are failing to prepare librarians for today's challenges, let alone the challenges of the future.
- Graduate programs in library schools should expand to a two-year curriculum.
- Graduate training in librarianship should be expanded to include instruction and practical experience in human relations and communications.
- Before becoming a professional, a librarian should serve an apprenticeship or participate in a field work experience.
- Librarians need training in "marketing."
- Are library schools preparing librarians to become good managers? Courses in public administration should be required.
- Students in library school must be prepared to fulfill the role of active information transfer agents, and must be recruited from those who have a realistic image of librarianship vs. those who see the profession as passive.
- Library schools are suffering from a lack of leadership.
- Library schools should have stiff entrance requirements, especially in terms of character and personality. Look for healthy, positive attitudes; aggressive not passive individuals.

American Library Association

- ALA should establish compulsory certification for librarians in all types of libraries.
- ALA should provide encouragement and support for those who need special motivation to excel.
- ALA must take the lead in establishing a definition of professional roles which will be accepted by a cross-section of librarians.

Cooperation and Communication

- Less distinction should be made between types of libraries. Librarians need to work together regardless of the type of library they work in.
- More emphasis needs to be placed on getting the information to the user regardless of the type of library it's in. More referrals need to be made.
- There is needless fragmentation of effort because librarians in different types of libraries do not work together and discuss problems.

PUBLIC ACCESS TO INFORMATION

- Dr. Blake has raised the barrier for providing equality of services . . . Equality of access is vital for [the] survival of society . . .
- If we really made consumer information available, powerful groups would be against libraries. [It] would affect economics.
- Are we in danger of sacrificing people needs (via closing neighborhood branches) in favor of funding machinery for sophisticated users?
- Should a library be all things to all people, especially those that have difficulty reading?
- User fees make libraries an elitist service.
- If we don't charge for services, there will be *no* access.
- How many library resources should be expended on reaching illiterates?

The above comments represent the spectrum of responses to the issues raised by Dr. Blake's thought-provoking paper. In general, participants were sympathetic to Dr. Blake's views; however, there were strong differences of opinion as to what and how much action ought to be taken to improve access.

As might be expected, the question of user fees, especially in public libraries, generated the most response. One discussion group commented:

- User fees—heated discussion! Majority feel no on principle but strong yes if it means that service cannot be available locally.

Other responses to the question of user fees included:

- Charging for services may stimulate awareness of need for funding.
- Fees for service—double or triple taxation. We must "sell" our services to those who fund us, not to the patron.
- There should be fees for certain types of users (e.g., industry).
- Information should be a public utility—free! Thus, government should fund the agency which provides public utility.
- Librarians should take over control of databases with heavy government subsidies in order to avoid user fees.
- User fees for services to business do not seem to be in accord with public access to information for *all.*
- Why not a sliding scale of fees?

On the question of the library being an elitist service, a majority of the conferees agreed that there were still segments of society which were not adequately served; they vigorously denied that this is the result of a lack of commitment to service. Two groups observed:

- We did not really agree with Dr. Blake that the information public libraries are giving is for the elite . . . Common in libraries we know are consumer information centers, auto repair manuals and pattern book centers.
- Access is becoming a problem because of budgeting expenditures. Are we going to sacrifice service to existing patrons to develop programs for the nonuser?

Among the conferees, the general position on access seemed to be:
- Our obligation is to find out what information is needed by our whole community and see that they get it.

What are the barriers to equal access?
- There are various types of barriers to library access: physical, indifference, levels of materials, punitive measure, privacy invasions, psychological, etc.

How can the barriers be removed? Some librarians felt that this had to be accomplished outside the library.
- We feel the need for legislation allowing open access to information necessary to the public to make human life more human.
- Librarians must get involved in developing social policies which assure that all users will have access to the information they need.

What should libraries do or change to meet the needs of those currently not served?
- Access may be bringing the material where the user is (e.g., prison) as well as bringing what they want.
- Examine hours, location, materials acquired, methods for distributing materials, and advertising. Then adapt all to community patterns rather than sitting back and waiting for people to come in the library.
- Find out where successful attempts to improve access have been made and replicate them.
- Develop access for underprivileged by making classification and notation schemes simpler so the library is easier to use.
- We must develop more meaningful ways of delivering information to groups with special needs, for example, video-tapes.
- If published information is too complex for the average man, can the library write popularizations or commission others to do so?
- Services and information packages must be redesigned to be usable to the illiterate.
- Have the library invite specialists on areas of information needed by patrons into the library to give information—particularly in legal or medical matters.

- Open access to the library by advertising on UHF, FM or CB.
- Identify what the library is best equipped to do; then refer the patron to the agency that can handle his need better if the library is not equipped to do it.
- The problem of servicing the poor is too broad for librarians alone. There is a need to work with others such as social workers, priests and ministers, police officers and teachers as a team to really help.
- Hire PR specialists. Certainly library PR is in a bad state.
- Publicize library's role as a provider of information.
- Resource sharing among libraries is an important aspect of getting information that they need to people.

What about the American Library Association and public access?

- Leadership from the Association has been negligible if not detrimental.
- ALA should identify programs for the "illiterate" and make them known to the profession.
- ALA needs a library advocate to make the public aware of public access.

Other comments which were stimulated by Dr. Blake's paper included:

- Libraries are more than information centers. They also provide books for recreation. We must not forget this aspect of our service.
- This session brought many issues and few answers.

CONCLUSION AND RECOMMENDATION

There is little doubt that those individuals who participated in the program felt that it was extremely beneficial to them. They welcomed the opportunity to participate actively in the annual conference. Whereas ordinarily programs are structured in such a way that most of those in attendance are necessarily passive participants, it was virtually impossible to avoid an active role in the Issues and Answers Program.

If one were to draw out the three or four themes that ran most consistently throughout the comments, one would have to mention:

- a serious uncertainty about the role of the librarian and, ergo, the library in our modern society
- a continued malaise about library education and what is perceived as its basic inability to produce graduates equipped to deal with today's library world

- a deep-seated fear of the uncertainty of the future which is brought on by changing economic conditions, rapid technological advances and ongoing social upheaval
- exasperation with the lack of planning and coordination which they feel takes place in the library world and the feeling that libraries have little say in charting their own course.

A logical next step in the process begun by the 1977 President's Program would be for the Association to plan a series of similar programs in the future. These programs could be conducted at the annual ALA conference or cosponsored with state and/or regional associations and conducted at their annual conferences. The programs would focus on one or two issues only. Papers presented at the sessions would focus on developing strategies to deal with the issue in question.

The 1977 Issues and Answers Program made an admirable start by bringing together nearly 1500 individuals and giving them the opportunity and challenge to focus in on some of the more vexing problems which the profession is facing. It would be interesting to observe the comments and suggestions which would come forth from a group of people brought together specifically to generate ideas about methods of dealing with these issues, to make recommendations for action.

The Detroit Conference may have been, through the President's Issues and Answers Program, the first step in a new approach which ALA could take to benefit from the collective imagination and interest of its membership.

Index

Compiled by Sanford Berman

AACR. *See* Anglo-American Cataloging Rules.
AASI. *See* American Association of School Librarians.
AECT. *See* Association for Educational Communication and Technology.
ALA Cataloging Code, 13
AT&T. *See* American Telegraph and Telephone Company.
Academic Institutes, 1-2
Academic Libraries, 38, 41, 52, 63, 66, 81, 89, 96-7
Access To Information. *See* Information Access.
Accreditation Standards, 82
Adelson, Marvin, 75-6, 78
Adult Education. *See* Continuing Education.
Advocacy. *See* Social Advocacy.
Affirmative Action, 40
Afro-American Librarians, 39
Afro-Americana Collections, 41
Age of Jewett, 19
Air Conditioning In Libraries, 68
Allerton Park Institute (20th), 65-6
Alliance of Information and Referral Services, 100
American Association of School Librarians, 83
American Association of School Librarians. Right To Read Committee, 109
American Challenge, xvii
American Library Association, 29, 36, 40, 42, 69, 83, 113, 117, 120
American Library Association. Committee on Accreditation, 83
American Library Association. Council, 103
American Library Association. Intellectual Freedom Committee, 29-30
American Library Association. Reference and Adult Services Division, 25, 105
American Library Association. Washington Office, 104
American Television and Radio Archive, 104
Anglo-American Cataloging Rules, 13, 15-16, 18
Apprenticeships, 117
Appropriate Technology, ix
American Telegraph and Telephone Company, 101
Arizona State University Library, 65
Aronofsky, Julius S., 52
Arrogance In Journalism, 7
Arrogance In Librarianship, 8
Assessing Community Information and Service Needs, 108
Association for Educational Communication and Technology, 83
Atherton, Pauline, 23
Atkinson, Hugh C., 64, 71
Audio-Visual Library Services, 22, 29
Auto Repair Manuals, 119
Automated Cataloging, 16-17, 21
Automated Circulation Systems, 69
Axford, H. William, 65, 71

Baker, Augusta, xv
Baker, D. Philip, 97, 104

Sanford Berman is Head Cataloger of the Hennepin County Library, Edina, Minnesota.

Baldwin, Paul E., 21, 23
BALLOTS, 17, 68, 74
Baltimore County Library, 65
Bank Automation, 58
Bar Codes, 25
Baumol, William J., 52, 64, 68, 71
Beckermann, E. P., 83
Belair, Robert R., 106
Bell, Daniel, xvii, 1, 9, 11, 87
Bender, David R., xv
Bendix, Dorothy, 37, 44
Benge, Ronald, 38-9, 44
Berninghausen, David, 37, 45
Berry, John N., 69, 71
Bibliographic Control Problems and Organizational Change Issues . . ., 23
Bibliographies, 89
Bibliotheca Universalis, 13, 19
Bierman, Kenneth J., 21, 23
Bilingual Library Services, 10
Black Americana Collections, 41
Black Librarian in America, 39, 45
Black Studies, 41
Blake, Fay M., xii, 86-93, 95, 104, 118-20
Bloomquist, L. L., 106
Bloss, Meredith, 104
"Blue Collar" Workers, xvii, 88
Blumenthal, Thomas, xii, 26, 36-46
Bodleian Catalog, 13
Boissé, Joseph A., xiii, xix, 110-21
Bone, Larry Earl, 43, 45, 64, 71
Book Catalogs, 13, 16, 21-2
Book Prices, 66
Book Sales, 67
Bovay, Sue, 104
Bowen, William G., 61
Boyle, Deirdre, 22-3
Boyle, John M., 104
Branch Libraries, 44, 96, 99, 105, 118
Braverman, Harry, 88
Braverman, Miriam, xiii, 83, 94-109
Breivik, Patricia Senn, 71
British Museum Catalog, 13, 19
Broderick, Dorothy, 103, 105
Brogan, Denis, 5
Brong, Gerald R., 22-3
Brooks, Jean S., 83
Brooks, Rae, 105
Brown, Eleanor Frances, 93
Brown, Lester R., 76, 79
Brown, Norman B., 66, 71

Brown University Library Catalog, 14, 18
Brownrigg, Edwin Blake, 69, 71
Bruer, J. Michael, 69, 71
Brutality In Children's Media, 103
Buckman, Thomas R., xii, 47-62, 114
Budgeting. *See* Library Budgeting.
Bundy, Mary Lee, 80-81, 83
Bureau of the Census, 34
Bureaucracy, 1-2, 5-6, 10, 99, 101
Burgess, Thomas K., 21, 23
Burton, Robert E., 67, 70-71
Busha, Charles, 106
"Business Mentality" In Librarianship, 92
Butler, Brett, 22-3, 25, 105

CBS. *See* Columbia Broadcasting System.
CLSI, 69
Cable TV Communication. *See* Video Communication.
Campbell, Patty, 105
Cancer Information, 90
Canyon, Jim, 105
Card Catalogs, 16, 22-4
Carter Administration, 54
Carter, Bradley D., 21, 24
Carter, Jimmy, 6, 70
Case, Robert N., 83
Casey, Genevieve M., 97, 105
Catalog Card Production, 14
Cataloging Codes, 13, 15-16
Cataloging Reform, 119
Cataloging Staff, 16
Censorship, 37, 42, 102-03, 115
Census Bureau. *See* Bureau of the Census.
Central Cities. *See* Inner Cities.
Central Intelligence Agency, 34
Centralization, 2
Certification of Data Bases, 34
Certification of Librarians, 117
Chapin, Richard E., 71
Chaplan, Margaret A., 71
Cheatham, Bertha M., 42, 45
Chelton, Mary K., xv
Chicago Public Library, 43, 95
Child Exploitation, 102-03
Childers, Thomas, 81, 83, 99, 105
Children and Television, 102-03
Children's Library Services, 42-3, 84, 103-04, 108

Chisholm, Margaret E., 81, 83
Christofferson, Rea, 65, 71
Church of Scientology, 101, 106
Churchill, Winston, 34-5
Cicero, 11
Circulation Systems, 21, 25, 69
Citizen Action, 1, 26, 29
Citizen Participation and Public Library Policy, 84
Civil Rights Commission, 34
Clasquin, F. F., 66, 71
Class Action Suits, 1, 26
Classification and Subject Index for Cataloging and Arranging the Books and Pamphlets of a Library, 18
Classification Systems, 14, 16, 105, 119
Classism in Librarianship, 91-2
Clerical Workers. *See* "White Collar" Workers.
Cleveland Public Library, 86-7
Client Relationships, 80-81
Collection Development Policy, 66-7, 70, 96
Collective Bargaining, 65-6
College Level Examination Board, 80
College Libraries. *See* Academic Libraries.
Columbia Broadcasting System, 8, 104
Columbia University Library, 14
COM Catalogs, 21-2
Coming of Post-Industrial Society, xvii, 9, 87
Commercial Vendors. *See* Vendors.
Communication and Identity, 38-9, 44
Community Policy Boards, 43
"Community Standards" Doctrine, 102
Computerized Cataloging. *See* Automated Cataloging.
Computerized Circulation Systems. *See* Automated Circulation Systems.
Computerized Learning, 2-3
Computers, 2, 14-17, 20, 22, 52-3, 57-8, 64, 86, 97, 112, 116
Computers In Information Data Centers, 24
Conant, Ralph W., 44-5
Conference Board, 53
Confidentiality of Records, 102
Confrontations, 113
Conroy, Barbara, xviii
Conservatism In Librarianship, 36
Consumer Information, 43, 57, 87, 118-19
Continuing Education, 28, 40-41, 112, 116
Copyright, 101, 103-04
Corporations, 76, 89, 101
Cost Benefit Analysis, 70
Costs. *See* Book Prices; Information Costs; Library Costs; Periodical Prices.
Crawford, Miriam, xv, 37
"Crisis Management," 64, 111
Croneberger, Robert B., 105
Crooks, Joyce, 106
Cuadra, Carlos, 109
Cuadra, Mary Fishburn, 109
Cultural Contradictions of Capitalism, 11
Curley, Arthur, xiii, xv, xvii, xviii-xix, 36, 45
Curriculum Alternatives, 83
Cutter, Charles Ammi, 13, 18

Dade County Citizens Information and Service Program, 100
Dain, Phyllis, 42, 45
Dallas Public Library, 80
Darling, Richard L., 65, 72
Data Bases, 17, 20, 23, 34, 68, 90, 94-6, 118
Deahl, Thomas, 105
Decision-Making, 3, 34, 38, 75-6
De Gennaro, Richard, 21, 23, 63, 66, 72, 82-3, 96, 105-06
Dehumanizing Technology, 111-12
Denver Public Library, 64
DeProspo, Ernest R., 84
Detroit, 5
Detroit Public Library, xviii, 64, 69
Detroit Public Library TIP Program, 29
Dewey, Melvil, 14, 18
DIALOG System, 95
Digital Computers. *See* Computers.
Dillon, Martin, 20, 24, 95, 106
Disabled Persons' Library Services, 98
Discrimination In Employment, 34

126 *The Information Society: Issues and Answers*

Dodd, James B., 106
Domestic Council Committee on The Right of Privacy, 59-61, 108
Doms, Keith, 68
Donahue, Joseph, 81, 83
"Dossier Society," 100
Dougherty, Richard M., 22, 24, 106
Douglas Aircraft Company, 14
Downs, Robert B., 81, 83-4
Drucker, Peter, xvii
Drug Information, 43
Dunatov, Elaine Tisch, 109
Dunlap, Connie R., xv

Eastman, Dan, 105
Echelman, Shirley, 81, 84
Economic Change, xii-xiii, 47-74, 114-15, 121
Economic Growth, 54-5
Economic Indicators, 55-9
Economic Policy, 54
Economics of Academic Libraries, 61, 71
Economies of Scale, xii, 51
Edison, Thomas, 11
EDITEC, 95
Education, xvii, 1, 3, 57, 63, 97
Education Policy, 1, 89
Educational Technology, 20, 22
Elitism/Elites, xiii, 2, 9, 91, 94-5, 98, 113, 118-19
Elrod, McRee J., 22, 24
Ely, Donald P., 83
Energy Conservation, 68
Energy Crisis, 26, 34, 67-8
Energy Policy, 54
Enoch Pratt Free Library, 69, 81
Environmental Policy, 54
Environmental Protection, 34, 63
Equal Access To Education, 97
Estabrook, Leigh, xii, 26, 36-46
Estrogen Information, 90
Ethical Standards, 4, 11
Ethnic Library Services, 10, 41, 99, 107
Ewart, Geraldine Sydney, 106

Facsimile Transmission, 2
Factory Workers. *See* "Blue Collar" Workers.

Fass, E. M., 106
Fast, Elizabeth, xvi
Federal Aid To Libraries, 33-4, 36-7, 69, 71
Federal Data Bases, 34
Fees. *See* User Fees.
Feiste, K. L., 106
Feminism, 40
Ferguson, Douglas, 67, 72
Ferragamo, Ralph C., 69, 72
Field Work, 117
Fines. *See* Library Fines.
Finland, 90-91
Firschein, Oscar, 106
First Amendment, 8, 100, 102-03
Fisher, Paul L., 106
"Floating Information Librarians," 115
Foil, Patti Sue, 21, 24
Folcarelli, Ralph J., 69, 72
Ford Administration, 59, 101
Formula Budgeting, 67, 70
Fourth Amendment, 100
Francis, D. Pitt, 70, 72
Frantz, John C., 43, 45
Fraser, Walter, 39
Free Library of Philadelphia, 67
Freedom, 77
Freedom In A Rocking Boat, 62
Freedom of Information Laws, 30, 32-3, 100-01
Freiser, L. H., 81, 84
Freud, Sigmund, 40
Fussler, Herman, 21, 24

GNP. *See* Gross National Product.
Galbraith, Kenneth, 9, 89
Galvin, Thomas J., xii, 64, 72, 80-85
Gardner, Jeffrey J., 21, 24, 94, 106
Gay Rights, 37
Geller, Evelyn, 103, 106
Gesner, Konrad, 13, 16, 19
Gilbert, Frances, 105
Gold, Steven D., 70, 72
Goldstein, Seth, 107
Gonzalez, M. Q., 106
Gorbey, Lucy, 37
Gotsick, Priscilla, 108
Government Information, 59, 100-01
Grosch, Audrey N., 22, 24

Gross National Product, xvii, 50, 55-6
Grove Press, 102
"Gutenberg Technology," 12
Guthman, Judith Dommu, 44-5

Handicapped Persons' Library Services, 98
Harman, Joyce R., 25
Harris, Michael H., 19, 42, 45
Harter, Stephen, 106
Hayes, Robert M., 77, 79
Heilbroner, Robert L., 61, 88
Heim, Kathleen M., 39
Hennepin County Library, 29
Higher Education, 3, 41
Hilmark United Corporation, 86
Hilton, Howard J., 86-7
Hirsch, Fred, 54
History of Cataloguing and Cataloguing Methods, 1100-1850, 19
Holt, Raymond M., 72
Horny, Karen, 23-4
Hospital Libraries, 98
Houston Public Library, 29
How To Use The Freedom of Information Act, 106
Hughes, Nola, 105
Human Capital, 1, 87
Human Relations Training, 117
Human Rights, 27
Human Services, 99-100
Human Use of Human Beings, 62
Humphrey, M. Moss, 107
Humphreys, James, 107
Hyde, Thomas, 13

I & R Services. *See* Information and Referral Services.
Ihrig, Alice B., xvi
Illiteracy/Illiterates, 3, 9, 43-4, 86-7, 118, 120
Illuminating Engineering Society, 68, 72
Immroth, Barbara, xii, 80-85
Impact of Online Retrieval Services, 109
Improving Access to Library Resources, 106
Independent Learning: The Role of Public Libraries, 84

Indiana Information Retrieval System, 98
Individualized Education, 3
Industrial Laboratories, 1
Industrial Revolution, 15
Inflation, 51, 63-5
Information Access, ix, xii-xiii, 3, 29-30, 49, 86-109, 118-20
Information and Referral Services, 28-9, 42, 44, 80-81, 96, 99-100
Information Costs, 48-9, 55, 57, 59
Information Economy, 62
"Information Explosion," ix, 57, 59
Information For Action, 93
Information Industry, 8, 56, 60, 89, 95, 101-02
Information Needs, ix, xiii, 9, 78, 89-92, 98-100, 107-08, 119
Information-Poor in America, 105
"Information Society" (Parker), xvii
Information Systems and Networks, 109
Information Transfer, xii, 25, 75-7, 99, 101, 115
Injustice, 6
Inner Cities, 26, 29, 44, 63
Inquiry Report, Kanawha County, West Virginia, 107
Institutional Libraries, 98, 107
Intellectual Freedom, 29-30, 42, 92, 100, 102-04
Interlibrary Loans, 17
INTREX. *See* Project INTREX.
Irby, Jane, 95, 104
Isaacs, Norman E., xi, xxii, 4-11
Island Trees Case, 42

Japan, xvii, 9
Jewett, Charles Coffin, 13-15, 19
Job Information Centers, 29
Jones, Clara Stanton, ix-x, xv-xvii, 35, 37, 43, 45
Jones, J. F., 21, 25
Jones, Wyman, xvi
Josey, E. J., xi-xiii, xv-xix, 39, 45
Journal Prices. *See* Periodical Prices
Journalism, 4-5, 7-8

Kamisar, Hylda, 107
Kanawha County, West Virginia, 102, 107

Kenney, Brigitte L., 22, 24, 99, 109
Kent, Allen, 84
Kies, Cosette, 107
Kilgour, Frederick G., xi, xv, 12-19, 21, 24, 111-12
Kimmel, Margaret Mary, xiii, 80-85
Kingsbury, Mary E., 82, 84
Kittel, Dorothy, 107
Knapp, Patricia B., 84
Knowing Your Community, 108
Kochen, Manfred, 93
Kohut, Joseph J., 70, 72
Korfhage, Robert R., 52

LSCA, 27, 69, 98-9
Labor and Monopoly Capital, 92
Labor Force. *See* Work Force.
Labor Unions. *See* Unionization.
Lacomb, Denis J., 22, 24
Lacy, Dan, 44
Ladendorf, Janice M., 81, 84
Ladenson, Alex, 96, 107
Lady Chatterley's Lover, 102
Langston Hughes Library and Cultural Center (Corona, New York), 100
Laser, David, 107
Latino Library Services, 10
Law, 6
Learmont, Carol L., 65, 72
Legal Aid, 6
Lemke, Antje B., 40, 45
Librarian As Learning Consultant, 84
Librarians' Roles, xiii, 75-85, 98, 114-16, 120
Libraries and the College Climate of Learning, 84
Libraries As Community Centers, xi, 10
Libraries As Educational Institutions, 2, 80-2
Libraries As Primary Institutions, 1, 89
Libraries In The Streets, 107
Library Advertising, 10, 119-20
Library and Information Service Needs of the Nation, 61, 107
Library Architecture Preconference Institute (1974), 68

Library Automation. *See* Automated Cataloging; Automated Circulation Systems; Library Technology.
Library Automation: The State of the Art II, 23
Library Bill Of Rights, 37, 103
Library Budgeting, 27, 51, 64, 67, 69-70, 96, 113
Library Cooperation, xiii, 2, 17, 34, 41, 67, 81, 96-8, 117, 121
Library Costs, xii, 21, 50-52, 64, 66-9, 96, 112, 114-15
Library Education, xiii, 27-8, 39-40, 72, 89, 112-13, 117, 120
Library Employment, 65, 82, 111-12
Library Fees. *See* User Fees.
Library Fines, 67
Library Funding, 2, 21, 27, 31-4, 37, 44, 50-51, 63, 69, 96-9, 114-15, 118
Library Goals Objectives, 28, 37, 43, 64, 78, 82, 112
Library Issues: The Sixties, 38, 45
Library Legislation, 31-5, 69
Library Manpower: A Study of Demand and Supply, 85
Library Networks, xi, 2, 12, 16-17, 21, 30, 34, 51-3, 67, 97-8
Library Networks, 1976-77, 25
Library of Congress, 98
Library Personnel, 22-3, 44, 50-51, 64-6, 111-12, 116
Library Planning, xiii, 41, 43, 67, 81-2, 111, 121
Library Productivity, 15-16, 21, 51, 64-5
Library Public Relations, 10, 113-14, 119-20
Library Records, 102
Library Resource Sharing. *See* Library Cooperation.
Library Response To Urban Change, 43, 45
Library Salaries, 40, 65-6
Library Schools. *See* Library Education.
Library Service to the Disadvantaged, 93
Library Services and Construction Act. *See* LSCA.

Library Services To Children. *See* Children's Library Services.
Library Services To Disabled Persons. *See* Disabled Persons' Library Services.
Library Services to Ethnic Groups. *See* Ethnic Library Services.
Library Services To Latinos. *See* Latino Library Services.
Library Services To Poor People. *See* Poor People's Library Services.
Library Services to Prisoners. *See* Prisoners' Library Services.
Library Services To Seniors. *See* Seniors' Library Services.
Library Services To Spanish-Speaking Persons. *See* Latino Library Services.
Library Services To Teen-Agers. *See* Teen-Agers' Library Services.
Library Services To The Disadvantaged. *See* Poor People's Library Services.
Library Staff. *See* Library Personnel.
Library Technology, xi, 12-25, 51-3, 64, 68-9, 82, 92, 111-12
Library Visibility, 10, 113-15
Lieberman, Irving, 22, 24
Lifelong Learning. *See* Continuing Education.
Lighting In Libraries, 68
Lippmann, Walter, 5
Literacy, 3, 10, 44, 87, 99, 109, 115
Literacy and the Nation's Libraries, 109
Livingston, Lawrence G., 21, 24
Lobbying, 29, 32
Lockheed Development Corporation, 95, 98, 106
Lowe, Thomas C., 106
Lowrey, Anna Mary, 83
Lucioli, Clara E., 107
Luck, Carolyn, 105
Lyman, Helen Y., 109
Lyman, Richard W., 41, 45
Lynch, Beverly P., 98, 107

McAllister, Desretta V., xii, 80-5
McAnally, Arthur M., 84
McCauley, Elfrieda, 70, 72
McGee, Rob S., 21, 25

McGrath, William E., 70, 72
Machlup, Fritz, 55
McKloskey, Judith, 108
McLean, Polly, 107
Magazine Prices. *See* Periodical Prices.
Mai Lai Cover-Up, 30
Malinconico, S. Michael, 22, 24
Management Training, 117
Manipulation, 2, 77
Manual Cataloging, 21
Marcus, M. J., 108
Marcus, Matityahu, 64, 68, 71
Marcuse, F. L., 102, 108
Markuson, Barbara Evans, 73
Marquis, Rollin, xi, xviii, 1-3, 22, 24, 26, 93
Martin, Allie Beth, xv, 84
Martin, Lowell A., 43-5
Martin Luther King, Jr., Hospital Library, 98
Martin, Susan K., xi, 20-25
Martinez Smith, Elizabeth, xvi
Matarazzo, James M., xii, 80-85
Mavor, Anne S., 84
Mazer, Norma Fox, 103, 108
Media Conglomerates, 8
Media Personnel In Education, 83
Media Programs: District and School, 83
Memphis Public Library, 64
Menopause Information, 90
Meritocracy, 2, 9
Merton, Robert, 61
Metropolitan Libraries. *See* Urban Libraries.
Metropolitan Library Authority, 96
Meyers, Duane H., 108
Microcomputers, 22
Microforms, 2, 21-2, 72, 86
Middle Ages, 15
Minicomputers, 22
Minneapolis Public Library, 67, 95
Minnesota Health Science Libraries, 98
Minority Librarians, 39-40, 82
Mobility. *See* Social Mobility; Upward Mobility.
Model Cities Legislation, 99
Molz, Kathleen, 44-5
Monopolies, 101
Monroe County Library System, 100, 104

Monteith College Library Experiment, 84
Moon, Eric, xvi, 45
Morgan, Jane Hale, 63, 73
Muckrakers, 5

NCLIS. *See* National Commission on Libraries and Information Science.
Nassau Public Library, 29
Nation State, the Multinational Corporation, and the Changing World Order, 79
National Bureau of Standards, 106
National Commission on Libraries and Information Science, 21, 25, 30, 89, 97, 99, 107-08
National Conference on Social Welfare. I & R Round Table, 105
National Education Association, 107
National Information Policy, 30, 33-5, 55, 59-61, 101-02
National News Council, 7-8
National Program for Library and Information Services, 25
National Science Foundation, 99
Negativism In Librarianship, 8
Neier, Aryeh, 106
Neighborhood Communications Centers, 109
Neighborhood Information Centers, 81, 109
Neighborhood Libraries. *See* Branch Libraries.
Networks. *See* Library Networks.
New Industrial State, 9
New Librarianship, 37, 46, 77, 79
New Rochelle Public Library, 68
News Media, 7-8, 104
Newspapers, 4, 7
Nitecki, Danuta A., 21, 25
Nitecki, Joseph Z., 21, 25
Nonformal Education, 26, 32
Norris, Dorothy M., 19
Nyren, Karl, 45, 65, 67, 73

OCLC, 16-17, 21, 68
OCLC in Retrospect, 25
"Obscenity," 102
O'Halloran, Charles, 69, 73

Ohio College Library Center. *See* OCLC.
Ohio Public/Institutional Library Cooperation, 98, 107
Ohmes, Frances, 21, 25
On-Line Bibliographical Services, 16-17, 21-2, 68, 94-7
On The Construction of Catalogues, 13, 19
Ordover, Janusz A., 61
Outreach Programs, 28-9, 37, 44
Overhage, Carl F. J., 25
Owens, Major, xii, 26-35, 100, 108, 113

PPBS, 70
Paley, William S., 8
Pallet, Dorothy, 107
Panizzi, Anthony, 13, 19
Parker, Edwin B., xvii, 54, 57-9, 61
Participatory Management, 38, 40, 64
Patron Relationships, 80-81
Peace, 27
Pearson, Karl M., 22, 25
Peninsula Library System Community Information Project, 95
Penland, Patrick R., 80, 84
Pentagon Papers Case, 30
Performance Measurement, 71
Periodical Prices, 64, 66, 96
Perlmutter, Edith L., 95, 104
Personal Consumption, 55-6
Perspectives on Organizations, 61
Phinazee, Annette L., xv, xvii
Photocopying Machines, 12
Pings, Vern M., 37, 46
Plan For Information Society, xvii
Plotnik, Art, 68, 73
"Plus Ça Change" (Shera), 36, 46
Pocket Calculators, 58
Pollution, 37
Poole, William F., 14, 19
Poor People's Library Services, 9, 43-4, 91-2, 119-20
Porat, Marc Uri, 56
"Pornography," 30, 102
Portteus, Eleanor M., 84
Possner, Karen B., 99, 109
Post-Industrial Society, xi-xii, xvi-xvii, 1-3, 87-8
Post, Joyce, 99, 105

President's Commission on Obscenity and Pornography, 102
Pressure Groups, 1
"Prime Market" Approach, 91-2
Printed Catalogs. *See* Book Catalogs.
Prison Libraries, 99
Prisoners' Library Services, 99, 105
Privacy, 2, 77, 100-02, 119
Private Sector, 1, 30, 34, 48, 92, 94-5, 101
Problem Solving, 96
Professional Education, 3
Professionalism, xii, 80-85, 114-16
Profit Motive/Profits, 89, 91-2
Programmed Learning, 2
Project INTREX, 20, 25
Proletariat, 88
Provencher, Lauri, 100, 108
Public Information Access. *See* Information Access.
Public Libraries, 4, 30, 42-4, 51-2, 63-4, 72, 80-82, 95-100, 105-07
Public Library Association, 82
Public Library In Non-Traditional Education, 83
Public Library In The Network Mode, 105
Public Sector, 1, 30, 48, 92, 95
"Publishing Explosion," ix
Publishing Industry, 74, 101
Pyhrr, Peter A., 70, 73

Quality of Life, 78, 104

RASD. *See* American Library Association. Reference and Adult Services Division.
Racism In Librarianship, 39
Racism/Racism Awareness, 42, 92, 103
Rand Corporation, 99
Randal, Judith, 93
Ray, Gordon, 53
Rayward, W. Boyd, 42, 46
Reading Guidance, 81
Recession, 27
Reference Librarians, 84, 98, 115
Reich, David L., 83
Reid, Marion T., 65, 73
Reitman, Allan, 100, 108
Rembar, Charles, 102, 108

Remote Access To Information, 2
Research Corporations, 1-2, 89
Research Libraries, 24, 64, 66, 74, 96
Research Libraries and Technology, 24
Resource Sharing. *See* Library Cooperation; Library Networks; Shared Acquisitions; Shared Cataloging.
Reston, James B., 7
Reynolds, Maryan E., 21, 25
Rhoades, James B., 101, 109
Right of Privacy. *See* Privacy.
Right To Information/"Right To Know," xiii, 42, 91, 100-01, 119
"Right To Read," 30, 42
Right To Read and the Nation's Libraries, 109
Rights. *See* Gay Rights; Human Rights; Library Bill of Rights; Privacy; Right To Information; "Right To Read."
Ringer, Barbara, 104, 109
Robbins, Jane, 81, 84
Roberts, Donald, xvi
Rochester County (New York) Library System, 100
Rodgers Report, 59-60
Rohlf, Robert H., 64, 73
Role of Public Libraries in Independent Learning, 84
Rosenblatt, Roger, 62
Rugh, Archie G., 105
Rules For A Printed Dictionary Catalogue, 13, 18
Rural Libraries, 105

SDC. *See* System Development Corporation.
San Diego Information Center, 100
Sannwald, William W., xii, 63-74
Scannell, Francis X., 73
Schiller, Anita, 39-40, 46
Schleph, Frederick A., 70
School Libraries/Media Centers, 41-2, 51-2, 63, 70, 81-2, 89, 97, 103
School Library Manpower Project, 82-3
Schuman, Patricia Glass, xiii, xv-xvii, 37-8, 46
Schumpeter, Joseph, 87
Science and the Modern World, 19

Science-Based Industry, 1-2, 89
Science Policy, 1, 89
Seniors' Library Services, 99
Serebnick, Judith, 103, 109
Serial Prices. *See* Periodical Prices.
Servan-Schreiber, Jean Louis, xvii
"Service Economy," xvii, 1, 88
Serving Youth: Communication and Commitment in the High School, 41, 46
Sexism In Librarianship, 39-40, 89
Sexism/Sexism Awareness, 42, 92, 103
Shapiro, Lillian L., 41, 46
Shared Acquisitions, 2
Shared Cataloging, 16-17
Shaw, George Bernard, 11
Shera, Jesse H., 36, 46, 82
Shields, Gerald R., xii, xv, xxii, 75-9
Siegel, Ernest, xvi
Slanker, Barbara, 95, 109
Slaughterhouse Five, 103
SLICE, 97
Sloan Foundation, 24
Smith, Elizabeth Martinez. *See* Martinez Smith, Elizabeth.
Smith, G. M., 38, 46
Smith, Jessie Carney, 41, 46, 81, 85
Smith, Ruth S., 109
Smithsonian Institution, 13
Snobbery In Librarianship, xiii, 91
Social Advocacy, 1, 26, 29, 75, 116
Social Change, xii, 26-46, 75, 113-14, 121
Social Justice, 78
Social Limits To Growth, 54
Social Mobility, 1-2
Social Policy, 1, 98, 104, 119
Social Responsibilities and Libraries, 38, 46
Social Responsibility, 29-30, 36-44, 78, 103, 113-14, 118-20
Social Rights, 1
Social Security Information, 87
Social Services. *See* Human Services.
Solar Energy, 68
Soledad Prison Inmate Library Committee, 99
"Songmy: Human Imperative" (Braverman), 105
Space Information Center, 34
Special Libraries, 52, 81-2

Spigai, Frances G., 22, 25
Stallings, C. Wayne, 109
Standards For Accreditation, 83
Status Quo, 39, 44
Steepleton, Judith, 63, 73
Steffens, Lincoln, 5
Stoffle, Carla J., xiii, xix, 110-21
Strategy For Public Library Change, 82, 84
Stuart-Stubbs, Basil, 67, 73
Subject Cataloging, 13-14, 16, 105
Subscription Rates. *See* Periodical Prices.
Summit, R. K., 106
"Sunshine Laws," 30
Suominen, Elina, 90-91
Supermarket Automation, 58
Supreme Court, 102
Swartz, Roderick, xv
System Development Corporation, 95

Talking Books, 107
Tarbell, Ida, 5
Technical Education, 3
Technical Services Librarians, 116
Technological Change, ix, xi-xii, xvi, 14-15, 23, 53, 56-8, 76, 82, 86, 94, 111-14, 121
Technological Unemployment, 16, 18, 112
Technology In Libraries. *See* Library Technology.
Teen-Agers' Library Services, 41, 46, 85, 103-05
Telecommunications, 2, 20, 22, 52
Telephone Reference Service, 115
Television Programming, 9-10, 102-03
Temple University Library, 25
The Information Place. *See* Detroit Public Library TIP Program.
Tillitt, Harley E., 14
Timidity In Librarianship, xiii, 91
Tinglum, John H., 68, 73
TIP Program. *See* Detroit Public Library TIP Program.
Toro, Jose O., 84
Torrance, J. S., 68, 74
Totten, Herman, xvi
Toward A National Program for Library and Information Services: Goals for Action, 108

Trend Toward Partnership, 107
Tropic of Cancer, 102
Troy-Miami Public Library, 68

U.S. Bureau of the Census. *See* Bureau of the Census.
U.S. Central Intelligence Agency. *See* Central Intelligence Agency.
U.S. Civil Rights Commission. *See* Civil Rights Commission.
U.S. Constitution. *See* First Amendment; Fourth Amendment.
U.S. Library of Congress. *See* Library of Congress.
U.S. National Bureau of Standards. *See* National Bureau of Standards.
U.S. Supreme Court. *See* Supreme Court.
Union Catalogs, 15-17
Unionization, 40, 64-6, 112, 115
Universities, 1-2, 89
University Libraries. *See* Academic Libraries.
University of British Columbia Library, 22
University of Chicago Library, 25
University of Michigan Library, 70
University of Minnesota Library, 22
Upward Mobility, 1-2, 87-8
Urban Libraries, 40, 42-44, 96-7, 105
User Fees, 21, 34, 49-50, 69, 75, 89, 92, 94-5, 114, 118-19
User Studies, 82

Vagianos, Louis, 20, 25
Vanderbilt University. TV News Archives, 104
Vavrek, Bernard, 105
Veaner, Allen B., 20, 25, 68, 74
Vendors, 22, 68, 94-5
Vickers, Geoffrey, 57
Vico, Giovanni Battista, 6

Video Communication, 2, 9-10, 22, 58-9, 86, 119
Videodiscs, 58
Vietnam War, 26, 30, 63
Violence In Children's Media, 103
Visibility. *See* Library Visibility.
Vonnegut, Kurt, 103

Wanger, Judith, 109
Wasserman, Paul, 37-8, 46, 77, 79-81, 83
Wax, David M., 21, 24, 94, 106
Ways, Max, 62
Wedgeworth, Robert, 37, 69, 74, 91
Weeding Policy, 66, 96
Weibel, Kathleen, 39-40, 46
Welfare Programs/Recipients, 26, 29, 87
What Black Librarians Are Saying, 39, 45
"White Collar" Workers, xvii, 88
White House Conference On Libraries, xii, 30-35
White House Conference on Libraries Advisory Committee, 28-9
Whitehead, Alfred North, 18-19
Wiener, Norbert, 47, 62
Williams, Martha, 95-6, 109
Willison, I. R., 64, 74
Women Librarians, 39-40
Women's Health Information, 90
Women's Movement, 40
Work, 88-9, 111-12
Work Force, xvii, 1, 55, 87-8

Yin, Robert K., 99, 109
Yonkers Job Information Center, 100
Young Adult Library Services. *See* Teen-Agers' Library Services.

Zero-Based Budgeting, 70
Zurkowski, Paul, 94-5, 109